Workshop in a book

Embellished Bras
basic techniques

Dawn Devine ~ Davina
with photography by Barry Brown

About the Author

Dawn Devine ~ Davina is the author of several books on the subject of designing and making Middle Eastern belly dance costumes. Her acclaimed first book, *Costuming from the Hip* (1997), has been a continuing international best seller among the dance community. Other titles include *From Turban to Toe Ring* (2000), *Bedlah, Baubles and Beads* (2001), and her latest booklet, *Style File* (2002). She has published numerous articles in dance publications and maintains a website with a quarterly e-zine called *Costumer's Notes*. She performs and teaches in Northern California.

About the Photographer

Barry Brown is a freelance photographer living in Northern California. With a particular interest in landscape, he can often be found roaming the Sierra Nevada and Yosemite National Park.

Barry also teaches full-time as a computer science instructor at a local community college.

Stripe, the photographer's assistant.

Special Thanks

I would like to take a moment to thank the incredible group of people who have made this book possible. My editorial staff, Michael Hyde, Pat Cahill, Peggy Beanston, and Judy Devine, who have all made invaluable suggestions that have shaped the content and style of this book.

Thanks also go out to everyone who has ever participated in my "Stuff and Fluff" workshop, especially Madame X, Kathi Richards of Simply Stylish, and The Two Old Bags: Janie Midgley and Chris Proebstel. Over the years I have been blessed to have so many opportunities to bring this workshop to cities all over California and Nevada. Thank you!

The unsung heroes of project books like this are the vendors I've worked with collecting materials for this project. This includes Gaylene of Gaylene's Boutique (fabric and paillettes), Mary June of Aunty Magpie's Shining Hoard (magpie bra covers), Harry Saryoan for his incredible coins, Scheherazade Imports (Egyptian fringe), Artemis Imports (tribal jewelry), and Sugar Petals (appliqués). Thank you for providing the dance community with supplies, knowledge, and support.

And a super-special thanks for my writing partner and photographer Barry Brown. I knew we could do it!

2011 - And a super-special thanks to Jerry Case who reformatted *Embellished Bras* into this new size!

Table of Contents

A good chest lift (and nice posture) is worth a thousand bust pads.

Introduction

For more than one hundred years, since the first commercially made bra was available on the market, dancers and costume designers have been dreaming up new ways to decorate the trusty brassiere. Once the domain of belly dancers and Las Vegas showgirls, the embellished bra has become a staple garment for fashion and costume designers. Social acceptance of innerwear as outerwear has allowed the bra to become more than just a supportive piece of lingerie. Bras encased in sumptuous fabric and encrusted with jewels are now being paired with long skirts for eveningwear and as prom gowns.

Today, dancers from many different genres of performance incorporate the embellished bra into their costume ensembles. Competitive and exhibition ballroom dancesport Latin costumes often feature a two-piece embellished bra and skirt combination. Even a dancer simply heading out for a weekend evening at the local club might wear a filmy blouse over a decorated bra designed to be shown off.

No matter the ultimate venue for your embellished bra, this book provides the techniques and knowledge that can bring your designs to life. This method is broken down into four phases: buying a lingerie bra, making a pattern to cover it, stitching the cover onto the bra, and then embellishing it. This workbook breaks each phase into smaller, achievable steps, presenting them with illustrations, photos, and text.

This method uses only a few inexpensive sewing tools and simple hand sewing techniques. The bra you select as your base and the fabrics and materials you use to embellish the garment will determine the cost of the final garment. From simple bright cottons with inexpensive chainette fringe to sumptuous silks coated in rhinestones and dripping with bugle beads, this method is simple and effective.

Even if you have been making costumes for a long time, you may enjoy reading another perspective and might even pick up a hint or tip. There is no one "right" way to sew, but rather, different tricks and techniques that fill a toolbox of knowledge and skills. During any project, you pull from your assorted skills to find the one that will fit your needs at that moment.

Take a moment to read through this entire book. Collect the tools and purchase the supplies you will need to turn your design dreams of a beautiful embellished costume bra into a reality. You really can do it!

Classic Belly Dancer

The embellished bra and belt set is the uniform of the Middle Eastern belly dancer. Encrusted with beads, sequins, and rhinestones, this style of costume is worn by dancers who perform in restaurants and clubs world-wide. The dripping layers of beads emphasize her movements, so, even from a distance, the audience can see the subtle vibrations and tiny, precise isolations that are the hallmark of this dance style.

Tribal Belly Dancer

Unlike her sequined-and-rhinestoned cousin, the tribal belly dancer wears costume elements from around the world. Authentic imported textiles encrusted with embroidery, mirrors, and shells vie for attention with her layers of jewelry adornment.

Styles of Dance Costumes

Showgirl

The hallmarks of the showgirl style costume include exotic feather headdresses, lavish applications of sequins, and rhinestones over tiny embellished bras and thong G-strings. Just add mile-high heels and you are set to strut the finest stages.

Sambista

A direct relative of the showgirl, the Sambista costume takes many of the elements of the showgirl costume and emphasizes it. Sambistas pair their skimpy embellished bikinis with sturdy dance shoes capable of marching in Mardi Gras parades. Giant feather headdresses and shouler harnesses are added to dan-cers riding floats.

Gypsy Costume

The quintessential Hollywood image of a Gypsy dancing girl includes layers of ruffled skirts, bright colors, flowing scarves and the coin bra. Gypsy dancers appear in parades and historical events and can pop up in a wide variety of dance shows.

Latin DanceSport

For competitive or exhibition ballroom dancers, the embellished bra can be one of the foundation garments for a Latin styled costume. Coated with rhinestones and paired with a kicky, flirty skirt, these costumes sizzle on the dance floor.

The Method: An Overview

This method will take you from a plain lingerie bra, like the one pictured above, to a fabulously embellished masterpiece.

Making an embellished dance bra can be a long, painful process or one filled with creative joy. It is easiest to break it down into a four-phase project with creative possibilities at each step. Breaking it down like this makes the whole project more manageable and turns this long, intimidating process into a rewarding and fun experience.

Design

For many budding costume designers, the most challenging part is knowing where to begin. "Design" is not a single step that is performed at the beginning of the project. Rather, it is an unfolding process that takes place during all of the subsequent steps. The design will probably evolve and change as you make choices about materials and techniques. Design is that intangible, intellectual place where you set the stage for your new design to emerge from your dreams into reality.

Phase I – Select the bra

Perhaps the most critical step of all is finding a bra that fits well and possesses all the necessary features. In phase one, we address the structure of the bra and how that relates to the fit. Also included is a summary of the styles, shapes, and features that are easiest to convert and transform into a lovely costume.

Phase II – Make the pattern

The heart and soul of this four-phase technique is making the pattern. This book takes you through step-by-step diagrams to help you create a pattern for your specific bra. Each bra is different, with wider or narrower bands, cups with different shapes and angles of tilt, and positioning of the straps. No one pattern can cover every bra, but with these simple techniques you can make a custom pattern for your bra base.

Phase III – Sew the cover

You'll never be slave to the colors and fabrics available in the lingerie department again! This phase of the book shows you how to take the pattern you made in Phase II and use it to completely encase your bra in sumptuous fabrics. Elegant beaded fabrics can quickly transform the humble bra into an exciting dance costume.

Phase IV – Embellish

This phase can be creative and exciting or tedious and dull. There is a wealth of options for surface design and we can only scratch the surface. However, we have presented a menu of options and examples that can help you design your own embellished bra.

Skipping steps

This book presents each and every step of these phases. However, many dancers find that they like to skip a step or two. There is nothing wrong with picking and choosing which techniques you will use cover your bra. Throughout this book we have included notes where skipping a step can save you time and money.

Design

The bra is an important component of the dance costume. The design of the bra and belt needs to coordinate, integrate, or match. It is important to consider the total look of the costume, not just the bra. Here are a few approaches to create a unified look between the upper and lower portions of your costume.

Chose a style or theme – Selecting a theme or style instantly limits your choices and gives you a direction to move towards. If your style is Gypsy, then you know you probably won't be investing in a lot of rhinestones. If you are shooting for a flapper style, you will be using lots of layers of chainette. Picking your style first helps guide the rest of your design choices.

Use the same materials – The easiest way to create a uniform look is to use the same materials on both the bra and belt set. By simply covering the bra and belt base in the same fabric, you create a uniform look. Using the same surface design treatments results in uniformity.

Color – Work with the same color palette throughout the entire costume, including accessories such as headdresses, decorative sleeves and embellishments. Color is a very important design element and most designers strive to achieve harmony, contrast, and balance between differing tones.

Use texture – Even if your costume is all one color, you can use texture to create visual interest. Think of all the different surfaces, from smooth shimmer of rhinestones and the shine of sequins to the depth of velvet or gloss of satin. Use the same textures throughout your entire costume ensemble.

Create balance – Strive to create the same visual weight of the bra and belt set. If you have a large bust and full coverage bra cups, you might design a thicker belt. In addition, you might want to make thicker bra straps to maintain uniformity of design.

Repeat shapes – If you are cutting the shape of the bra cups, repeat the same shapes in the forms of the belt. Keep the rhythm of the garment harmonized by repeating details of the shape. If you use a circular center motif, repeat it on the bra with small circles and curves. Alternatively, if you are using angles on the edge of the bra, repeat them on the belt.

Repeat motifs – If you are using a geometric pattern, floral design, or organic motif, repeat the design on both the bra and belt. Remember to repeat the motifs on the front, sides, and back of the costume as well. Motifs don't have to be exactly the same. They can vary in size and shape, and color.

Fringe – Use the same type of fringe, and the same materials, but don't feel you always need to use the same length. Fringe on the lower half of your costume can be significantly longer than fringe on the bra.

For more specific information on the principles and elements of design, please refer to *Bedlah, Baubles, and Beads*, Part I, which focuses on design issues as they relate to composing an ensemble for Middle Eastern belly dance.

Design

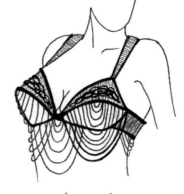

Design is all about answering questions and solving problems. In this case, we are addressing one problem: "How do I create the most beautiful cotume possible?"

There is no one simple answer. Instead, let's break this question down into smaller parts. As you step through this design exercise, answer the questions below in terms of your own costume. There are no right or wrong answers, just decisions that you, the designer, have to make to achieve your goals.

General questions

What is the "style" of the costume? Glitzy? Tribal? Gypsy? Flamenco? Other?

How will I decorate the bra?

What must be included to give the flavor I'm trying to achieve?

Is there a motif or color I can't live without?

What is my budget?

Can I afford to invest in the supplies I really want?

How much time do I have to spend on this project?

What is the venue? Where will I wear this costume?

Selecting the bra base

How much cleavage do I want to put on display?

Will I add padding to the bra?

How wide do I need or want my straps to be?

Will I be covering my bra? If not, what color bras are available?

Will I be using the existing bra straps?

Covering the bra base

How much work do I want to put into this project?

Do I want to bead the surface by hand or use pre-beaded fabric?

What colors will I be using for the fabric and embellishments?

What kind of fabric will I be using?

Do I want to add texture with a print or surface embellishments?

Embellishing the bra

How much time do I have to decorate this bra?

Do I enjoy sewing enough to fully encrust a bra?

Am I going to use fringe? Will I make it myself?

Where will the fringe be placed?

What colors will I be using in the surface design?

Are there new surface design techniques I want to try?

Design Croquis

One of the handiest little tools that professional designers use to help them create exciting new costume designs is the croquis. Invented in France during the rise of the fashion designer in the middle of the nineteenth century, this tool cuts down on the time and effort it takes to design by eliminating the need to produce the underlying figure. With these pre-drawn figures, designers simply sketch right over them. Here are several croquis to help you in your designing. There are several ways you can use these. The first is to simply photocopy a pile and have them ready for you sketching enjoyment. Alternatively, you can use lightweight sheer or transparant paper, such as tissue paper or pattern paper, to simply trace over the figure.

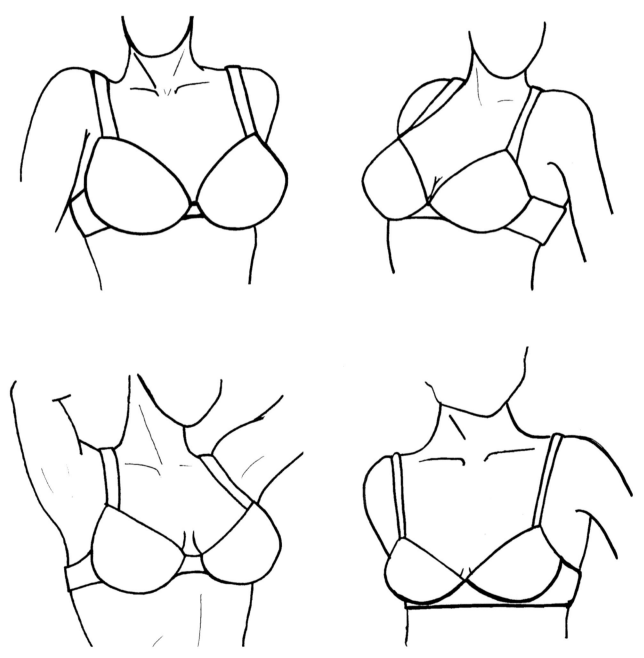

Phase I - The Foundation Bra

The Steps

1. Select a bra style
2. Determine your size
3. Go shopping
4. "Test drive" during fitting
5. Buy your lingerie bra base

Bra Myth: I have to tilt the cups!

Contemporary push-up- and plunge-styled bras are designed and manufactured with tilted cups. Just use the bra as-is — the tilt is already there!

Bra Myth: I have to buy one cup size larger!

If you plan on adding padding to your bra, then you may want to buy one cup size larger. However, as long as you don't pull your stitches too tightly, your bra should maintain its shape and form.

Once you have developed your design and have a drawing or sketch of your bra, it's time to go shopping! Look at the style you have drawn and figure out what kind of bra works best with your design concept.

A good dance bra has the following features:

- Underwires to maintain structural integrity.
- Firm, non-stretch cups.
- Light to firm padding to provide strength and shape.
- Styling that flatters your body and design goals.
- Excellent fit before deconstruction begins.

Buy the best you can afford

You don't want to invest lots of time and money into a bra that will fall apart after a few wearings. Dance is a vigorous activity that puts a lot of stress onto the garment. Inspect the bras you try on to make sure that stitches are firmly attached and secure. Hanging threads are a sure sign of poor construction, so look at all the seams and give them a good tug to test for strength. Of course, control your strength! You don't want to rip bras apart in the store.

Test the features

Once you have a bra that has all of these characteristics, it is time to give it a test. Put it on. Try a few dance moves in the fitting room if possible, especially chest rolls, pops and lifts, and arm movements. If the bra stays put through a full range of dance motions, you probably have a good basis for further construction. Here are a few other ways to test the bra and see if it will work. When going out shopping for a bra, take a long a test kit including bra pads, a necklace, straight pins, safety pins, and sturdy ribbon.

- Pin a necklace to the bra during fitting and check the amount of sag and pull across the tops of the cups. Be careful not to damage the bra! Use sharp, thin, and long pins.
- Place the bra on a table, chair, or even on the floor. Look at it from all angles. Do the cups support themselves? If you lay a necklace across the bra cup, does the cup support it?
- Pull the edge of the cup. It should stretch very little and immediately snap back into shape. Test the underwires to make sure they don't bend or flex too much. Inspect the construction of the cups to make sure the seams are all sound and sturdy.
- If you are planning alternative straps, you can pin temporary ones onto your cups. This is especially important when using a strapless bra. Repositioning the straps can really change the look and function of a bra.

Have you found a bra you love?

Stock up! Bra styles, shapes, and fabrications change from season to season. If you find a bra style that works well for your figure and style, you may want to invest in several. Next time you run to the store to purchase a bra, that model may be long gone. If you have the money to buy more than one, pick up a spare. You'll be glad you did.

Bra Structure

The standard push-up bra is one of the most complex garments worn today. Only shoes are made from more individual parts and pieces. Bras are so complicated, in fact, that most seamstresses have never even attempted to make one from scratch. However, understanding the mechanics of the bra structure will help you build a stronger, more comfortable, and shapely costume piece.

Underwires – These engineering marvels create a firm foundation for the cups. They act as the pillars in a suspension bridge, which provide a rigid structure for the suspended cups. The underwire needs to rest against the chest wall to stabilize the entire bra and keep the bra cups in place. Underwires need to be wide enough to wrap around the breast mound without poking either into the side of the breast (too narrow) or into the arm (too wide).

Chest band – This is the band that goes around the body, linking the bra cups and reaching around the back. Some styles of smaller plunge or push-up style bras only have a band at the back, and rely on a simple center tab to pull the cups together.

Center piece – In a partial-band bra, there is a separate center panel that holds the cups together. This can be a narrow band or a triangular-shaped piece of reinforced fabric. The size of the center piece determines the shape of the cleavage.

Bra straps – In a well-fitted bra, the straps don't provide lift but, rather, control bounce and sway of the bust and hold the top of the bustline against the chest wall, keeping everything in place.

Bra cups – Perhaps the most complicated part of the bra is the cup. There are only two major ways of creating a bra cup: it can be molded from foam using chemicals and heat to create the shape or the bra cup shape can be created by stitching together pieces of fabric. While you cannot make a molded bra at home, it is possible to build a pieced-cup design.

Two-piece cup – The most common shape is the two-piece design. A single seam runs over the breast mound at the apex of the bust, which is usually in the vicinity of the nipples. The position and angle of the seam will create different stylistic looks in the foundation bra, but these are generally obliterated when the bra is covered and decorated.

Three-piece cup – The three-piece style of bra cup is often found in larger-sized and strapless bra styles. The added seam provides extra strength and can help with shaping. For vintage costume styles, a three-piece cup will give a more traditional 1940s or 1950s style shape.

Molded cup – This style uses heat to shape the cup. Molded bras come in a wide variety of shapes and styles. Make sure you select one that has an underwire! These bras come in larger sizes and are often called sweater bras, T-shirt bras, or lightly-lined bras.

Three-piece bra cup

Horizontal two-piece bra cup

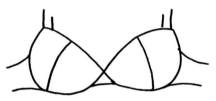

Vertical two-piece bra cup

A – Strap
B – Band
C – Cup
D – Center piece
E – Underwire

Bra Sizing and Fit

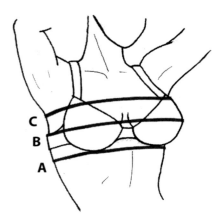

Use the diagram above as a reference when measuring your body. Don't pull too tightly on the tape measure. Rather, let it lay smoothly across your body. It may help to have a friend or a bra-fitting professional measure you.

One of the great mysteries in life is understanding how a bra should fit. According to statistics offered by the garment industry, more than 75% of American women wear the wrong size bras. Department stores and specialty lingerie shops offer bra-fitting services. Yet different companies use a variety of formulas for calculating your band size and cup size.

In this method you use three measurements: the rib cage, full bust, and upper bust.

Line A: Measure your rib cage just below the bust line. Add 4" or 5" to reach an even number. A measurement of 31", for instance, would be converted to 36".

Line B: Measure your full bust across the nipples at the fullest part of the bust line.

Line C: Measure the upper or high bust line. This is over your bust but just under your armpits.

Subtract the high bust measurement (B) from the full bust measurement (C). Using the chart to the left, find your cup size.

Underwires directly relate to the fit of the bra

Underwires – Without the structural integrity that the underwires provide, the bra structure would collapse under the weight of surface decoration, fringe, and other embellishments. Since it's the combination of the bra cups and the chest band that support the bustline, having well-fitting cups with the proper sized underwires is important. There are three dimensions for the underwires and cups to keep in mind when trying on bras.

Underwire width – The width of the cup should be wide enough to hold the bust. Every body is different. The breast mound for a 36B might be wider and flatter on one woman or narrower with more projection on another. Measure the width on your favorite bra to know what feels best on you.

Underwire height – Different bra styles have different underwire heights. Strapless bras have a U-shaped wire that is longer and creates a higher cup. A plunge bra or demi-bra style has a less dramatic curve and a shorter cup height.

Cup depth – This creates the shape of the forward projection of the cup away from the chest wall. The size and curve of the cup is somewhat predetermined by the shape and length of the underwire. However, the seaming or molding process can cause the cup to protrude more or less.

Bra Cup Chart	
C minus B	**Cup Size**
Less than 1"	AA
1"	A
2"	B
3"	C
4"	D
5"	DD or E
6"	F, DDD, or EE
7"	G, FF, or EEE

Helpful Hint

If you are having trouble finding a bra to fit, try to find cups that fit. Straps, strap placement, and the angle and shape of the band can all be adjusted, but fixing a cup is tricky. Take two of each bra into the fitting room with you. Hold a cup in each hand in the position they will take when made up into a bra. You may find the perfect cups. While swapping out the band is time-consuming, it can be done and straps are an easy adjustment to make. Buy for the size and shape of the cups!

Help! I can't find a bra in my size!

One of the great challenges for many ample-figured women is finding a firm-cupped bra in a larger than average size. While I have seen bras as large as 44DD in many stores, women who are larger endowed may find it necessary to shop at specialty bra shops. Frederick's of Hollywood has a custom bra-making service that can build bras in virtually any size. There are other companies available through the Internet that provide similar services. Alternately, you can build a bra yourself. Elan® Patterns offers styles for large-sized bras. Contact information for these and other companies is available in the resources list on page 62.

Bra Styles

Now that you know what parts and pieces go into the bra structure, here are some of the most useful and popular styles and features to use as a base for a costume bra.

Push-up bra – These are styles that are designed to bring the breasts together and lift them up. Theses bras feature narrower centers, angled underwires, and sculpted padding or pockets for removable pads.

Strapless bra – The firm-cupped underwire-style bra generally has a beefier, wider, and more supportive chest band, sometimes with boning for extra support. The wires are more U-shaped and provide a good deal of lift but generally doesn't create cleavage. Strapless models often come in much larger sizes than push-up bras.

Convertible bra – A similar style to a strapless, the convertible bra has moveable and removeable straps. Generally, convertible bras are designed with very firm, strong cup construction to handle the changing stresses of different strap positions. They are frequently designed with slightly angled underwires and a plunge effect that is more revealing.

Plunge bra – This style of bra is designed with V-neck style shirts and dresses in mind. It has triangular-style cups that create the strong V-line. The underwires are angled and dip low to meet at a very low center band. Straps are usually positioned more narrowly to help create a bit of cleavage.

Padded demi-bra – Demi simply refers to a shorter cup that reveals more of the bust mound. Demi's come in a variety of styles from demi push-ups to demi strapless and demi plunges. Demi bras are much more revealing, so make sure when contemplating a demi style that you try it on and make sure you have enough coverage to be comfortable in a public setting!

Balconette – This style of bra creates a "sling" for the breasts and is designed for square necklines. It brings the bustline together but doesn't provide extreme lift. The straps are often widely spaced and the underwires are more U-shaped. This is a good choice for creating a vintage-styled costume.

Triangle bra – The triangle style of bra, which is often used to make bkini swimsuits, is a good choice for a dancer with a small bustline. Triangle style bras have a very nice shape and give good coverage, but usually have short underwires.

Contemporary bras are available in a variety of colors, sizes, shapes, and styles. While you are shopping for bras, try on as many as you can. "Test drive" different cup and band sizes, as they vary between manufacturers. While you may be a 36C in one company's bra, you may find a 38B fits better from another. Only by trying on as many as you can will you find the perfect bra.

Fitting Tips

The center panel or band should sit right on the breastbone without any gaps. If your bra gaps away from the chest wall, the cups may be too small or the band too big.

The front and back of the bra should be straight across the back. If the back slides upwards at the center, the chest band may be too large or the cup size may be too small.

If your bust line is bulging out over the tops of the cups, the cups are too small.

The straps should not be supporting your bust line. That is the job of the chest band. If the straps are digging in, you are not getting enough support from the chest band and may need to select a style with a bigger or wider chest band.

Phase II - Making the Pattern

Pattern-making Steps

1. Trace the center piece
2. Select a strap style
3. Draft a pattern for the strap cover
4. Trace the bra band
5. Drape a pattern for the cup

Making the pattern to cover the bra is, perhaps, the most important phase in this technique. Not every bra needs every pattern piece. Some dancers like to purchase black bras and leave the straps and band black, embellishing only the cups. The straps can then blend in with other black garments, make a dramatic line across a nude back, or get covered with other costume pieces.

If your bra design is built up over a plain, solid, neutral color such as black, white, or red, you may try simply purchasing a bra in that color and skipping this step entirely. Many costumers I have known take the final fabric and drape it directly onto the bra. They follow the pattern-making steps with the final fabric, then simply stitch it down when they get it all into place.

So, why make a pattern?

Nearly every dancer I have talked to has been mystified by the pattern-making process. They either faithfully follow commercial patterns with slight modifications or they attack the fabric, committing to a good deal of wasted material. Making a pattern may seem like an unnecessary step, but it actually achieves several goals.

It saves money. Fabrics encrusted with beads and sequins can be quite expensive. However, this is the quickest and easiest way to embellish a bra. If you have a pattern for the bra, you can reduce the amount of fabric you waste through the draping process. This also means you can plan your layout in the most efficient manner.

It allows for precise positioning. Wildly printed or embellished fabrics can be tricky to position on the bra to make the cups match. When you have a pattern for the cup, you can lay the pattern down on your fabric and precisely position it over your design. Flip the pattern over for the other cup and repeat this process.

You can have perfectly aligned darts. Some dancers drape their fabric directly onto the bra. This technique works well but it can be tricky to line up the darts perfectly. The direction they point, the length of the legs, and the shape of the line can all vary. If the underside of your bra will show, using a pattern allows you to be more precise in dart placement.

You can cover several bras. If the bra you have selected is comfortable, fits well, and creates the shape you like, why not purchase several before the model goes "out of season" and disappears forever? By making a pattern for the bra cover, you can quickly and easily make multiple embellished bras.

They are a tool for planning the surface embellishments. If you are planning on doing surface beading, integrating a variety of small appliqués, or working with coins and tribal jewelry, you can use your pattern piece as a template to lay out your materials. This can be especially helpful during complex beadwork. Before you spend a lot of time and money, you can take your pattern to the bead store and plan your design.

This bra is a perfect example of how a store-bought bra can be transformed easily with a few simple additions. We loved the color of this bra, so we simply covered the upper part of the cup with a motif cut from black re-embroidered lace. A row of flirty tassel fringe emphasizes motion and repeats the color scheme. This bra could be paired with a ruffled skirt, a pair of tight black pants with red samba ruffles, or incorporated into a flamenco-themed showgirl or belly dance costume.

Pattern-making

This phase steps you through the pattern-making process. Pattern-making embraces several techniques and we will use three of the four major methods in this project. Since we are starting with a commercial bra, we are essentially building a pattern for a cover that completely encases the lingerie base. Because the foundation garment has dimension, it has curves that stick out and it stretches and gives.

Every bra is unique. Different parts of the bra are easier to pattern using different techniques.

Drafting – In this method, the pattern is built using using measurements of the garment gathered with a tape measure, ruler, and a pencil. Use the measuring tape to measure the pattern piece and transfer the results to the paper using a ruler. Drafting is used in our project to make the pattern to cover the bra straps.

Tracing – Since we are working from an existing garment that has a lot of complex curves, sometimes it's easier just to lay the garment onto a piece of paper and simply trace it. This method is less precise than drafting, but it is a good choice for places where there are tricky curves or a lot of stretch. The tracing method is used to make the pattern for both the center front and bra band.

Draping – This method is the most complicated but in many ways the most fun and rewarding. In this technique, a square of cotton cloth is gently manipulated with your hands and pinned into place to create a perfectly fitted pattern piece. The draping process uses more tools than drafting or tracing, adding scissors, pins, a tape measure, ruler, and pencil. The key to successful draping is keeping a firm, even pressure with your fingertips, avoiding drag lines by smoothing your hands over the surface of the fabric.

Flat patterning – While this is probably the most commonly used method for making a pattern, the flat pattern technique is unsuitable for our project. This method uses a fitted master block, called a sloper. The sloper is copied and then manipulated by adjusting its shape and configuration until a new design is achieved. Since every bra is different and no master pattern is available, we aren't going to use this method in this project. However, in my advanced bra workshop, we will take the pattern we have made here and manipulate it using this method to come up with some interesting variations.

Pattern-making is just a skill, yet many people feel intimidated by the process. If you find you enjoy this process you may want to take a class in pattern-making at your local community college, adult education, or sewing center. If you want to read more, there are several good resources on pattern-making at the back of the book.

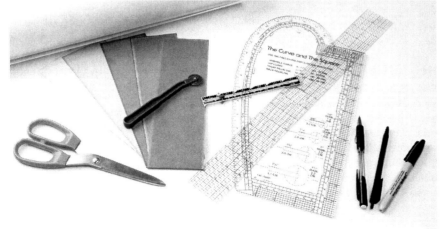

Pattern-making Tools
Roll of plain white paper
Paper shears
Tracing wheel and tracing paper
Hem gauge
Clear plastic ruler with grid
Designer's curve
Pens and pencils

Prepare the Bra

Grosgrain ribbon

Before you drape the pattern or cover the cups directly, prepare the bra for handling. The shape of the cups can become distorted when handled extensively, and it's a good idea to stabilize the upper edge of the cups.

Grosgrain ribbon

This is the secret weapon of the costume maker. Grosgrain (pronounced "grow grain") ribbon has a number of properties that make it an exceptionally versatile costuming component. It is very strong and durable. It is available in a variety of colors and several widths. But what makes this ribbon an excellent tool is its ability to resist stretching.

Grosgrain ribbon applied to the straps, the tops of the cups, and the center front provide the bra with added stability and support. Some costume designers take this one step further, using grosgrain ribbon to reinforce the line along which fringe or other heavy embellishments will be suspended. Many dancers add a row of grosgrain ribbon to the upper and lower edges of their bra bands as preventive measure against the elastic giving way during performance.

Adjust your shoulder straps

Before you begin any preparation to your bra, put it on and adjust the sliders. Move around, bend, stretch, and dance. Really test the limits of the bra and let the straps slide a bit until they are sitting at the most comfortable position that accommodates your motions but still provides good fit.

When the bra straps are perfectly adjusted, take the bra off and put a stitched tack below the sliders (see photo at left). This prevents them from moving after you have completely sewn the garment. If you plan on swapping out your bra straps for a pair of custom designed straps, you can skip this step.

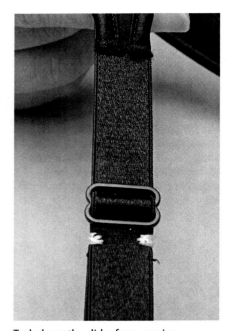

Tacks keep the slider from moving.

What about interfacing?

It is a good idea to reinforce a bra with heavy-duty interfacing. Interfacing helps the bra in two ways. First, it stabilizes the cups to keep them from further stretching and pulling. Second, it provides another layer that strengthens the bra and prevents stitches from popping through. This is especially important for bras you plan to embellish with heavy beaded fringe, jewelry, or coins. Wait until after you have your master bra cup pattern made so you can cut your interfacing to fit perfectly. You can find more information about applying interfacing on page 35. There are three styles of interfacing that I recommend.

Hair canvas is a product used by tailors. It's a scratchy, stiff interfacing that is very strong, so it is only applied to the outside of the bra. Because it's woven, it helps prevent stitches from pulling out through the foam or padded cup.

Heavyweight, non-woven, sew-in interfacing, such as Pellon®, can be found in most fabric stores and comes in white and sometimes black. It is inexpensive and easy to use, but not as good at preventing pull-through.

Medium to heavyweight woven interfacing is used to stabilize bodices for wedding dresses. This style of interfacing rivals hair canvas for its durability, but it is not as scratchy. The weaving makes this interfacing stronger, so even a medium weight will add a lot of support.

Helpful Hint

Some dancers leave the strap and simply lay one layer of grosgrain ribbon on the top of it. Select a color that matches the color of the bra or its covering. Then add some decorative element directly onto the grosgrain. If your bra has wide straps and is the right color, why not just stitch your emebellishments directly onto the strap?

Measure a length of 1" wide grosgrain ribbon an inch longer than the upper edge of your bra cup. Pin into place and fold the ends under.

Whipstitch the upper edge, beginning from the center and working out towards the straps. Although I am using white thread for demonstration purposes, match your thread color to the bra base or ribbon color.

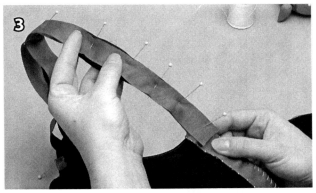

Measure the length of the straps. Sandwich the straps between two layers of grosgrain to add strength.

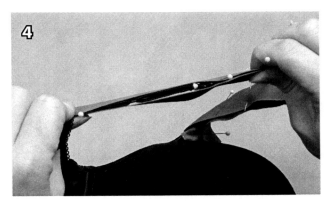

Make sure to measure the strap when pulled to maximum stretch.

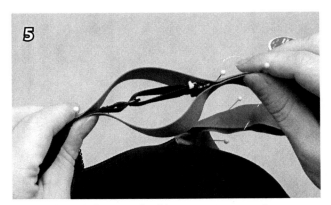

When released, the strap shauld return to its normal unstretched length.

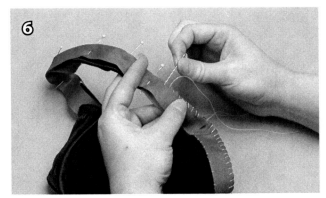

Stitch the two layers together using a whipstitch. Repeat all steps on the second strap. Make sure to stitch both sides of the straps.

Make Pattern for the Center Panel

The center panel of most plunge or push-up bras is quite narrow. They can vary from anywhere from a simple ½" band of ribbon to a 2" wide triangular panel. While front-opening bras can be effectively turned into an embellished dance bra, it takes more work. Bras that open in the front run a greater risk of popping open at inopportune times, especially during vigorous chest movements and shoulder shimmies.

The easiest way to make a pattern piece for the center is to trace it. This method allows you to make a pattern piece quickly and, since the piece is so small, tracing is a snap. Throughout the tracing process, try to keep the bra from moving.

What about front-closure bras?

Each front-closing bra has a unique system and there is no single reinforcing technique that accommodates each style. If your closure has a plastic hooking system, plan on swapping it out in favor of large metal hooks and eyes. This area is under tremendous stress during dance performances and a plastic hook might pop open or break under the strain. You can remove the closure and create your own using double thickness grosgrain ribbon and hooks. If you decide to stay with the closure that came with the bra, apply grosgrain to the top or bottom and stitch into place.

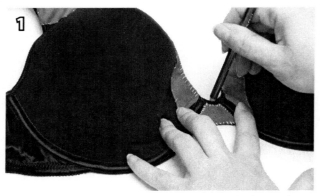

Lay the bra on a piece of blank paper. Position the bra so the band is pressed down against the paper. Trace the upper edge of the band first. Mark clearly where the center front panel or strip hits the cup.

Trace the lower edge of the band. Mark the corners where the cups attach to the center panel.

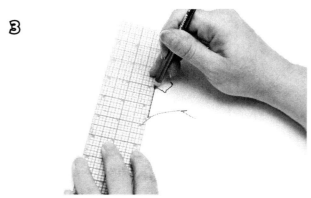

Connect the top and bottom lines on both sides using a ruler. The shape of this piece might wind up looking very different than the pattern shown above, depending on the particular bra you have chosen.

Mark a seam allowance of 1" all the way around the piece. The image above is not shown to scale

Make Pattern for the Strap Covers

If you plan on simply encasing the straps with grosgrain ribbon, you can skip this step entirely. If you are short on time, simply buy ribbon that matches or coordinates with your costume base. Then you can add your trim to complete the costume. This step greatly reducens the construction time and amount of sewing.

Depending on the composition of your covering fabric, there are two ways to cover the bra strap. The one-seam method requires a smooth or comfortable fabric. In this method, depicted in the photos below, the fabric is wrapped around the strap and a single seam is stitched up the underside.

Can I skip this step?

Because straps are linear design elements, you can choose to simply wrap them with a strip of fabric and stitch them into place. Many costume designers do this without cutting a separate pattern piece but, instead, measure and draw the shape directly on the fabric.

Cover the grosgrain directly

Another alternative to covering the straps is to simply apply your embellishment directly to the grosgrain ribbon or the bare strap. If your bra is already the right color, why do more work?

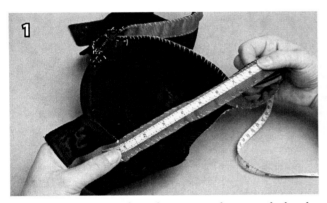

Measure your bra strap from the cup over the top to the band. Make sure to measure on the outside of the band across the top of the strap.

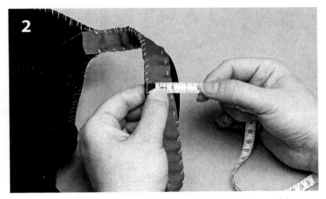

Measure the width of the strap. If the strap varies in width, measure the widest spot. In our sample bra, the strap is wider at the top of the shoulder and is wider than the grosgrain ribbon.

Draw a rectangle that is the length of the strap and 1/4" wider than the width. This added width is to accommodate the thickness of the bra strap.

Add an inch of seam allowance all the way around the bra strap. If your bra strap is narrow, use a smaller seam allowance.

Alternative Strap Options

Helpful Hint

When designing your bra, remember the back view is as important as the front. When selecting strap styles, think of how you plan on decorating the back of the bra. You may find that one of the styles works best with your design concept and surface embellishment plans.

Above – Use hook-and-eye closures like the ones above on halter-top and collar styles. Plan on an extra ½" of length to fold under for added strength.

Below – The bra for this demonstration is a convertible style. This style is designed to be worn either strapless or to have straps that hook on.

One of the easiest ways to customize a bra is by changing the shape of the straps. Building new bra bands can be a little tricky and reshaping the cups requires some advanced sewing techniques. Changing the standard straps to make a more decorative and distinctive style uses the same simple hand sewing techniques that reinforcing the existing straps uses.

Grosgrain ribbon is the key. Use a ¾" or ⅞" wide ribbon for the most comfort. Since you are swapping out the straps, you may elect to use a ribbon that matches the color of the rest of the bra cover. This will eliminate the need for covering the bra straps with yet another layer.

Designing the new straps

Prepare. Begin by getting your existing straps perfectly adjusted. You will be ignoring these straps, but it's essential that your bra sliders be positioned in the place that affords the best fit.

Select a strap style. There are several styles illustrated on the opposite page. Don't feel limited by these few suggestions. Experiment and play with a variety of design possibilities in your sketches.

Put your bra on. Measure from the band to the cup, following the line that the new straps will take. It helps to have an assisstant during this step. Write down your measurements.

If you are working alone, use a long length of grosgrain and pin it into place where you like on the band. Put your bra on and pull the ribbon over your shoulder and pin into place on the cup. Take the bra off and mark the two ends. This will become your pattern piece.

Prepare the straps. Grosgrain, while strong, needs to be reinforced before transformation into straps. With a sewing machine—or by hand—weld your grosgrain together with stitching. I like to use two layers of grosgrain for most sizes. For D cups or larger or on tribal bras with lots of weight, I use three layers.

Cut and sew the ribbons. Make sure to leave an inch on both ends. This will accommodate stitching into your bra cups and band. Use a firm whipstitch all the way around the ends for security and strength.

Halter style straps

Perhaps one of the most flattering bra strap styles is the halter. Halters pull the tops of the cups toward the center of the body, emphasizing cleavage. They also create a beautiful line across the chest. This is a style that many costume designers love and use for their ensembles.

However, halter straps can be very uncomfortable. The combined weight of the breasts, the embellished bras, and the centrifugal forces from vigorous moves are all channeled to the one small area where the strap crosses the back of the neck. Dancers with large breasts or bras heavy with lots of beads, coins, or jewelry should avoid the halter style. For dancers who do a lot of large or intricate chest, arm, or neck moves, the halter style may limit the range of motion. If you fall into either of these categories, you may want to skip the halter style for a more conventional shoulder strap style.

Halter front

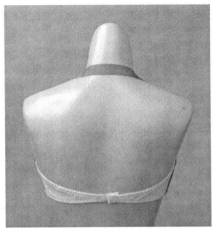

Halter back

Left – The halter style is a pretty choice for dancers with a B-cup bustline or smaller. When you design your halter, plan for a hook and eye opening. This will make getting into and out of your bra quick and easy. Be sure to use heavy-duty hooks!

Center row – These three strap styles are alternatives to the conventional H-back style. The V-back is a good choice for dancers who find their straps slip off their shoulders. The X-back provides maximum support and is an excellent choice for dancers with large breasts. The Y-back style most closely resembles a halter in the front, yet transfers the stresses of the cups to the back band.

V-back style

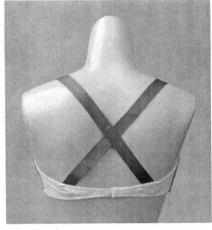

X-back style

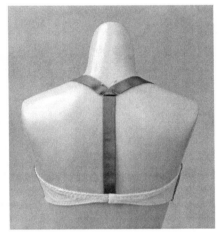

Y-back style

Collar front

Collar back

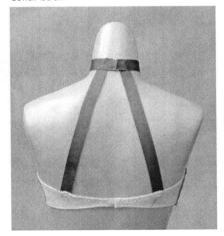

Left – A collar style like the one pictured will give you the opportunity to pull the upper edges of your bra cups in at the top, but still transfers the weight of your bra to the back band. In this style of bra, the collar can be heavily embellished to replace a necklace. This is one of the most complex styles to design. For the best possible fit, make the collar first, including the hook and eye. Pin your four straps to the bra, pull them up, and pin to your collar.

23

Pattern for Bra Band

Tracing is the easiest method for making the pattern for your bra band. All bra bands are different and your band may look thinner or thicker than the on the bra used in the photographs here. Tracing accommodates for the unique shape of your band.

Bra bands are held together by hooks and eyes. Most bras have rows of one, two, or three hooks, although larger and specialty bras may have many more. Our sample bra has three. To accommodate the widest variety of fit, most bras are adjustable with multiple rows of hooks. Because each hook and eye closure is slightly different, we will simply trace around the end when making the pattern. When it comes time to actually stitch the hook end, we will cut away part of the fabric to expose the hooks.

Can I make my own band?

Many dancers like to control the amount of stretch, the shape, and configuration of their costume by building their own bra bands. This is a more advanced technique that requires a good deal of sewing expertise. The next workshop book, *Embellished Bras: Advanced Techniques*, goes into detail on several methods for reworking the bra band. In a nutshell, there are two major techniques.

Build a band – You can use interfacing and grosgrain ribbon to build a sturdy, firm band that you then cover with your bra fabric.

Grosgrain ribbon or belting – This method is similar to swapping out the straps. Wide grosgrain ribbon or belting is shaped and stitched into place to serve as a band for the costume.

Lay your bra strap on a piece of paper with the outside of the cup facing up. Make sure the paper is wide enough to accommodate the bra strap when stretched to maximum length.

Flip the strap up and out of the way. Holding the cup in place, trace the outer edge of the cup between the top and bottom edge where the band connects to the cup.

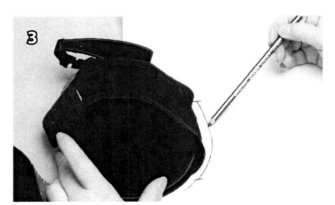

Mark the position of the top and bottom of the strap with a short cross line.

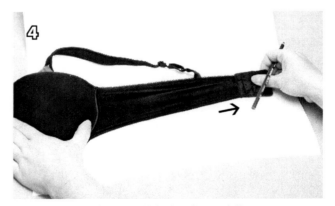

Holding the cup firmly, pull the band to its fullest extension.

While holding the hook end in place, release the bra cup. Trace around the hook end.

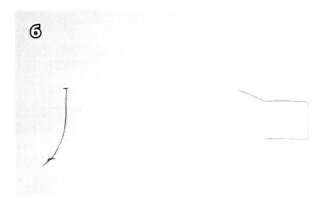

The traced lines should look similar to the illustration above.

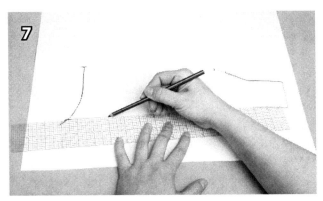

Use a ruler to connect the cup line to the hook end.

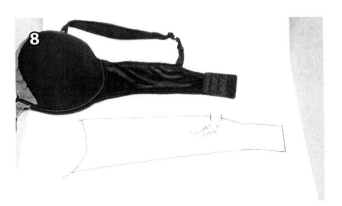

The resulting piece should look like the photo above.

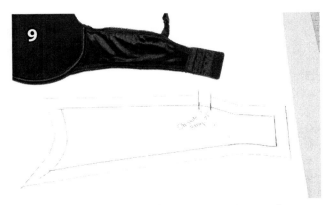

Add seam allowance around the entire strap. Use a wide allowance (5⁄8" to 1") to accommodate adjustments during the sewing process.

Label the final pattern piece. Include the bra model number for future reference.

Make the Bra Cup Pattern

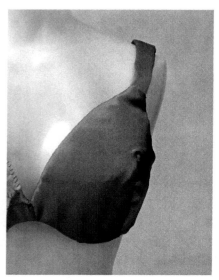

This is your goal: a lingerie bra smoothly covered with a fabric of your choice.

The heart and soul of this technique is the process of draping the bra cups to make a perfectly fitted pattern. Draping the cups is probably the most difficult and time-consuming part of the process. However, if you assemble the materials and pre-read the directions, it will go quicker.

What is draping?

In a nutshell, draping is a process that uses lengths of fabric which are eased, pushed, and pulled into a smooth, perfectly fitted shape. It takes two-dimensional fabric and turns it into a three-dimensional form. When the fabric, called a *drape*, is removed from the figure or object it covers, it becomes the basis for a pattern. The pattern makes it possible to re-create this drape in a more permanent form.

Draping tips

Here are just a few tips to keep in mind when working on this phase of the project. Draping may be completely new to you, but it's a very effective technique that anyone can learn and master.

Use your fingertips. Always smooth the fabric gently. Don't tug, stretch, or pull.

Never leave drag lines. If the fabric is pulled tightly enough to create long vertical lines, you have pulled the fabric too firmly. If drag lines appear, release the pins around in the area and smooth the fabric.

Use as many pins as you need. You will see from the photos that I use a lot of pins during this process. If your project begins to resemble a porcupine, you are probably doing it correctly.

Watch the grain lines. Woven fabric has a distinct warp and weft. The way the grainline falls will determine how smoothly the fabric will fall around the cup. Where the bias falls, the cup will more easily and smoothly sweep over curves. I use a gingham fabric to allow you to clearly see the direction of the grain.

Can I skip this step?

Maybe. Many dancers elect to drape their bras in the finished fabric. If you are planning on omitting the pattern-making step, follow this process from step 1 to step 25, then stitch the drape onto the pattern and repeat on the other side. However, making a pattern means that you will be able to quickly cut out both the cup covers and the lining pieces. If you intend to use heavy embellishments, you can also use the pattern to quickly cut interfacing pieces to further reinforce the bra cups.

If you plan on directly draping your final fabric onto the bra base, take extra care when clipping corners and trimming edges. You do not want to cut too deeply into the cloth. If you accidentally snip too far, the cut edge will show on the outside. If this happens, you may want to either consider redraping the cup or altering your decorative scheme to cover the offending slice.

Darts

Darts are used to transform a two-dimensional piece of cloth into a three-dimensional garment. The bustline is one of the most complicated to fit, and darts are essential to create a curved shape. Even though your bra may not have obvious dart lines, you will need to insert them in order to curve and fit the fabric to the bra.

Each bra is shaped differently and sometimes darts are not obvious. In two-piece or three-piece bra cups, the darts have been converted to seams. In molded bras, there may be no dart at all because the manufacturing process eliminates the need for shaping by molding foam over forms.

Dart placement rules

- The dart needs to point to the bust mound.
- The dart needs to start at an outer edge.
- The bigger the cup, the larger the dart.
- The longer the seam, the bigger the dart.
- Larger cup sizes may work better or be easier to handle with multiple darts.
- If you want the cup to appear smooth, plan to put the dart under your surface design.

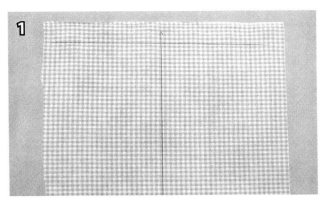

Begin with a square of woven cotton cloth. Draw the grain line on the fabric. In these photos, we used gingham to graphically illustrate the grain. Make the square of cloth 4" longer and 4" wider than the widest part of the cup.

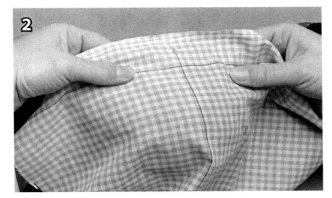

Position the center of the drape on the upper edge of the cup. Make sure the crosswise grain aligns with the upper edge of the cup.

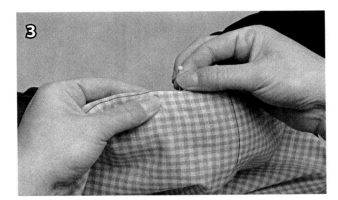

Fold the fabric over the edge, pinning the cloth down. Begin in the middle of the cup and work towards the center of the bra. Then go back to the middle and repeat the process, moving towards the strap.

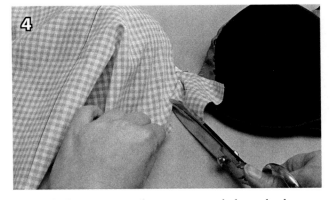

Where the bra cup meets the center, smooth down the drape and pin into place. Use a pair of fabric shears to clip into the cloth, aiming for the bottom edge where the cup and the center meet.

Bra Cup Pattern

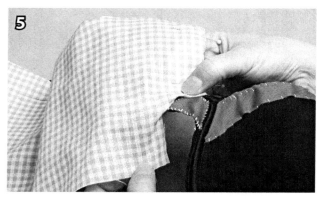

5 After clipping, you will be left with a tab of fabric. Take this tab and fold it under, creating a smooth, neat, folded edge. Pin into place.

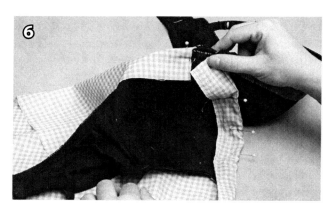

6 At the strap, cut into the drape, aiming for the spot where the strap meets the upper edge of the bra cup.

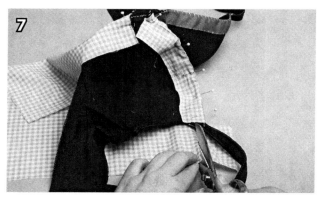

7 Cut into the drape to the point where the strap meets the side of the bra cup. This leaves a fairly large square of fabric.

8 Remove this square. Cut it off about an inch from the bra cup, at the same angle as the side. (Not shown: on the front of the cup, fold this seam allowance down and pin into place.)

9 Smooth the drape over the cup and pin along the side, moving from the strap downward, along the side of the cup. Flip the cup over and trim the excess fabric away, leaving an inch seam allowance.

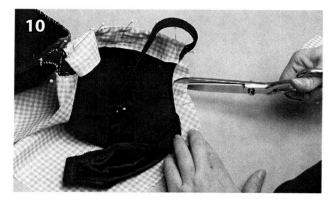

10 Snip this seam allowance approximately every inch, cutting almost to the edge of the bra. These cuts allows the drape to fit smoothly around the curve of the side of the bra.

Fold the drape over the side of the cup, pinning it into place. Be sure not to pull too tightly, which might distort the shape of the cup.

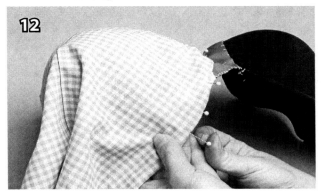

Flip the cup over and move to the center front. Gently smooth the drape over the cup, folding under the edge. Pin frequently. Go slowly and try not to pull the fabric. Instead, slide your fingers over the cloth, gently smoothing it into place.

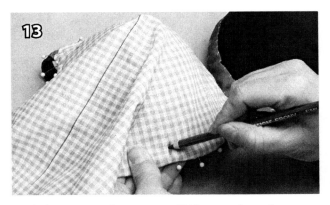

Mark the position where you would like your dart to be located. Use a pen or pencil to indicate the position of the lower edge of the dart leg. Use as many pins as you need to smooth this area into place.

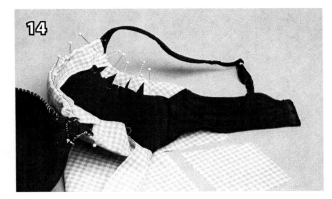

Smooth excess fabric towards the center front. Flip the bra and lay out the band. Remove excess fabric, cutting to the point where the band meets the lower edge of the cup. You will wind up with a wedge-shaped piece.

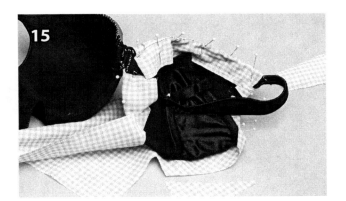

Flip the band up into the cup and trim the fabric, leaving a 1" seam allowance.

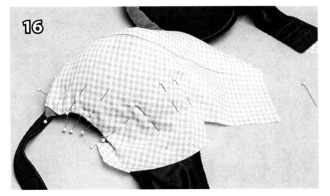

Flip the cup over to the outside. Smooth and pin the fabric into place along the bra band. Do not pin too close to the underwire.

Bra Cup Pattern

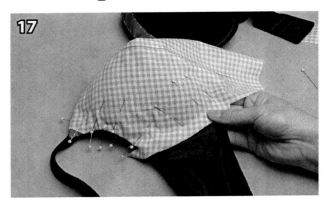

Neatly fold under the seam allowance and re-pin close to the lower edge. You may need to clip the seam allowance to allow it to lay smoothly.

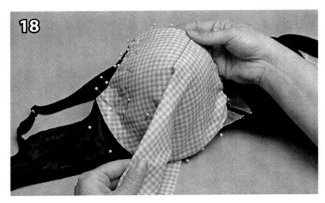

You now have a large fold or pleat of excess fabric. This forms your dart.

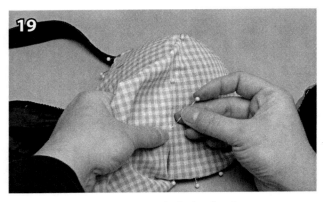

Gently smooth the fabric towards the bra band. Position a row of pins from the apex of the cup down to your mark. These pins should form a line that traces the position of the dart. Pin through both layers of fabric and not the bra cup.

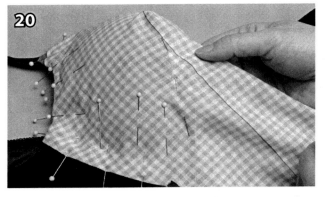

Fold the fabric towards the center. Notice that you can see the row of pins from this side. If the drape is not smooth, unpin and make adjustments as needed. This may take a few tries. The drape needs to lay smoothly with pins marking the dart leg.

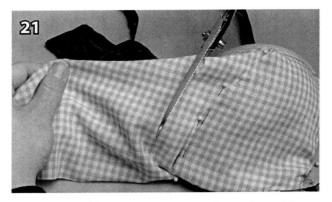

Remove excess fabric. Leave a generous 1" to 1 1/2" hem. The result should look similar to the next photo.

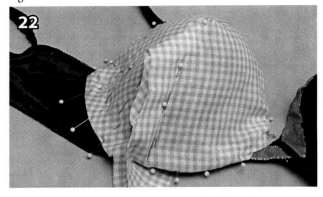

After trimming, this is what you should be left with.

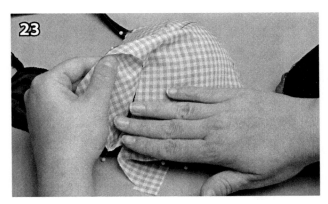

Unpin the dart. Gently use your hand to smooth the fabric from the front towards the bra band. Pin into place along the bottom edge of the cup.

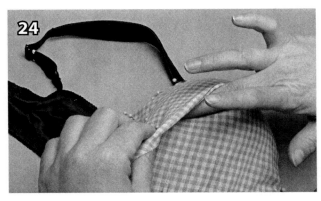

Fold the fabric over your finger to help make a smooth, clean edge. Slide your hand toward the tip of the dart while gently pulling the folded edge into place.

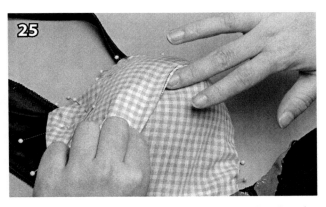

This should feel just like wrapping a package. Use the edge of your finger to create a smooth, neat fold at the apex of the bra.

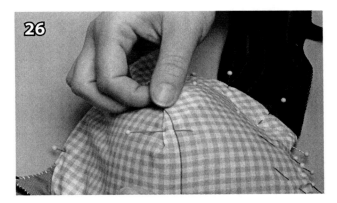

Begin pinning the dart just under the apex. As you work your way down towards the edge of the cup, you may find you need to adjust the fold. You want to create a smooth seam. Use as many pins as you need. This may take practice.

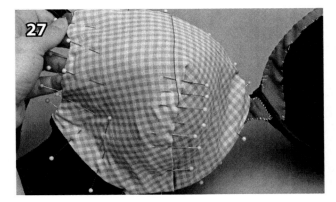

The final result should look like a straight line that reaches from the apex of the bra to the lower edge. Pause a moment here to make sure that you have no pulls or strain on the fabric. It should lay smoothly across the fabric.

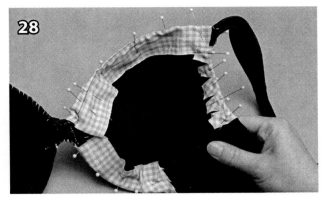

Flip the bra over and look inside the cup. Your results should look similar to the image above.

Bra Cup Pattern

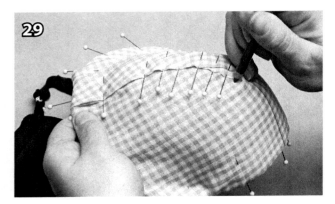

Trace the edge of your dart line with a soft pencil. Make sure that you mark both edges.

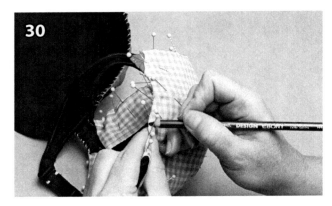

Continue to mark the outer edges of the bra. Use the side of a soft pencil to create a line along the edge. Make sure to go completely around the bra, including the places where the drape is folded under at the center front and along the band.

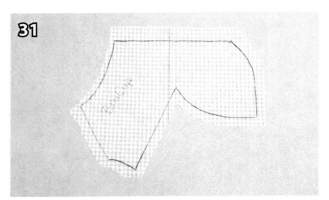

After you have traced all the edges, remove the drape from the bra and label. Your piece should resemble the pieces above.

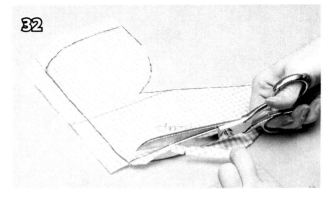

Remove the excess fabric by cutting along the line you have drawn.

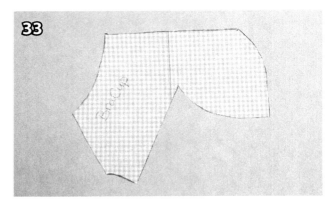

Your drape should look like this. If your bra has a small cup size, the dart will be smaller.

Lay the drape on a piece of plain paper. Use a weight to keep the drape from slipping as you trace it with a pencil.

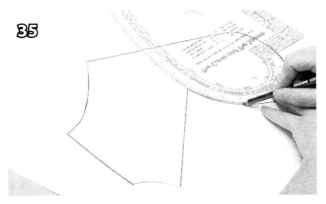

35

A pattern-making curve can help clean up and smooth the edges. If you cannot find a pattern curve in your local fabric store, any French curve for drafting or art will work.

36

Go over all of the lines to darken and smooth them.

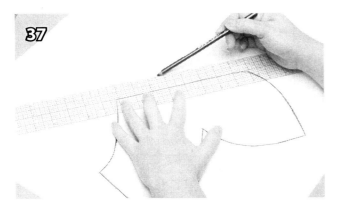

37

A see-through ruler makes adding the seam allowance easy. Add a one-inch seam allowance around the entire piece.

38

Label the pattern piece with the size and model of the bra.

39

Trim away the excess and your pattern is complete.

Your pattern piece is a handy design tool. Not only is it useful for cutting out the lining, interfacing, and fashion fabric, but it can also be used as a template for laying out the beading and other surface embellishments.

Label and store your pattern pieces in case you cover this same make and model of bra again. If you purchase a similar model and size, this pattern might work well with only a few minor adjustments to the shape of the dart and the position of the straps and center front. Put your pattern pieces into a labeled envelope and store it in your pattern collection so you can find it when you need it.

Phase III - Sewing the Cover

Order of Construction

1. Cut out all pieces
2. Add interfacing (if needed)
3. Cover the center front
4. Cover the Straps (if needed)
5. Cover the bra band
6. Cover the cups

The next step is sewing the bra covering. At this point, you should have your bra prepared and the pattern made. Sewing the cover can be tricky the first few times. You may want to sew a sample bra the first time. The key to effectively sewing the bra together is to stitch the pieces in the correct order. Although you can put together the bra in many different ways, this is the order of construction that has proven to me most effective.

The straps and the center front are base pieces. The straps get overlapped on both ends: in the front by the bra cups and in the back by the band. The bra cups are the last piece, as they overlap the straps, band, and center front. As you proceed, work from inner layer to outer layer. In this method, the bra cup is the last piece applied. That way all the raw edges are covered neatly.

Do I have to sew it by hand?

Some dancers try to cover their bra using their trusty sewing machine. They scootch around the underwires using their zipper foot and they squeeze their cups under their presser foot. While this can produce a sturdy bra, there can be some problems.

Cup distortion – When a padded, molded foam, fiber-filled, or pieced bra is pulled through a sewing machine, the cup becomes distorted. The fabric may get pulled during the sewing process which can cause the padding to bunch or shrink up. When you sew the bra by hand, you can control the tension of your stitches to prevent shrinkage and distortion.

Seam shows – When you stitch a bra with the machine, the stitches show on the outside of the bra. Some dancers cope by planning their trim to hide this stitching. Hand stitching is done entirely on the inside of the bra to create a smooth finish on the outside.

Control – When you are putting your cups through the sewing machine, you lose some of the control that you have when you are sewing by hand. The tension on the fabric from the feed dogs and presser foot can vary, as can the tension on the thread. The result can be uneven stitching. When you sew it by hand, you can see the surface that you are sewing better, you can flip the bra over, and have lots of pins in place as you sew.

What fabric is best to use?

Any dressmaker fabric can be used to cover the bra. Some fabrics work better than others. Stiffer, heavyweight fabric is easier for novice sewers to handle. Fabrics such as brocade, damask, dupioni silk, taffeta, and satin are easy to handle. Lighterweight fabric, sheers, and knits are more difficult to handle because they can cling or creep as you position the fabric on the bra cup.

Knit fabric with Spandex can be challenging. Don't be afraid of this fabric. Just keep in mind not to stretch it, especially when making the cup. If you inadvertantly pull it across the bra, you can distort the cups. This may not be obvious at first glance. As you work, use your fingertips to feel the shape and contours of your cup. If you see any draglines or if you feel ripples in the cup walls, you have pulled the fabric too tightly. With knits, you need to go slowly and check frequently to avoid over-stretching.

Materials for Building the Bra

This project requires just a few supplies to construct an embellished bra:

Padded underwire bra
Interfacing
Grosgrain ribbon

Outer fabric and lining fabric
Thread
Design elements to embellish the bra

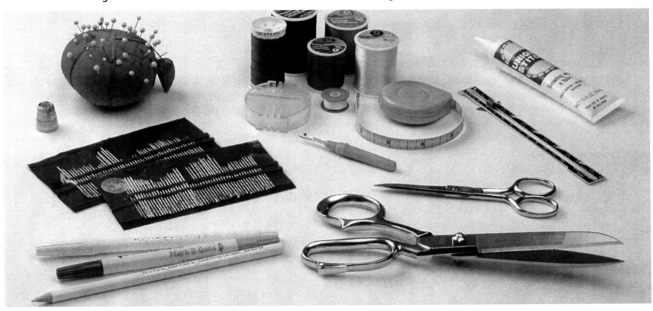

Tools for Sewing

There are very few specialized sewing tools needed for this garment. In your sewing supplies, you may already have everything you need to get started.

Needles
Pins
Thimble
Beeswax

Marking pens and pencils
Tape measure
Seam ripper
Thread

Fabric shears
Hem guage
Fabric glue
Tracing wheel

Cut the Pieces

Before you can begin sewing, cut out all of the pieces you need to cover your bra. Prepare your fabric by pre-washing your materials. If you plan on hand-washing the final garment, hand-wash prior to construction to test color fastness. You may want to stitch up a sample square with your surface embellishments as well.

You may want to experiment with laying out your fabric to conserve material. If you are using a specialty print or fabric with a design, you might want to play with pattern placement to show off the material to its best advantage. You may want to use a contrasting thread to baste around the pattern piece.

For a fully covered and lined bra, you will need to cut out the following pieces.

Main Fabric

Center front	cut one
Bra band	cut two
Straps	cut two
Bra cups	cut two

Lining

Center front	cut one
Bra band	cut two
Bra cups	cut two

Interfacing

Bra cups	cut two, no seam allowance

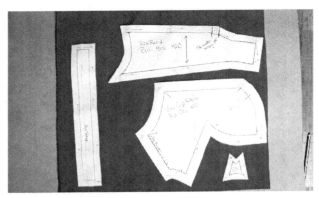

Lay out your pattern pieces on your fabric. In this case, the fabric is solid, so the fabric is aligned with the grain. However, if your fabric has a complex design, you may want to place your pieces so the pattern is positioned perfectly on your bra.

Trace onto interfacing without seam allowances. Use a tracing wheel and tracing paper so you don't have to damage your pattern. Then again, if you will never use this pattern again, you can simply cut away the seam allowance.

Cut out the fabric using sharp fabric shears. Dull scissors can damage the cloth. A rotary cutter is a good alternative. Start with the smallest pattern piece and work up to the larger ones.

As you can see in this detail, I have placed my pins in the seam allowance to prevent the pins from marring the fabric. Test your fabric and make sure that pin marks won't show before pinning through it.

Apply Interfacing

This layer is optional. If you plan on embellishing your bra with heavy, beaded fringe, tribal jewelry, or heavy coins, interfacing will help stabilize and reinforce the bra cup. For bras that are simply being covered with a decorative fabric and a row of braid, ribbon, or other lightweight trim, you can skip this step to save time.

All bras give somewhat, no matter how firm the padding. Adding this layer of interfacing helps stabilize the cups and prevents additional stretching. If you have a larger or fuller bust line, this step is essential to maintain the shape and form of the bra cup.

Use a heavyweight, non-fusible interfacing for this process. If your bra is black, you may want to try to locate black interfacing. Resist the urge to use fusible interfacing. While fusible interfacing could be used, don't iron it onto the bra because most bras don't react well to heat. Lycra, nylon and rayon are all very heat sensitive and molded foam cups can melt and become distorted, even with relatively low temperatures.

Some dancers like to use two layers—one on the outside and one on the inside—to create a sturdy sandwich effect. If you plan on doing this, you may find you need to trim your interfacing a little shorter all the way around on the inside piece. Simply pin into place and then carefully trim away excess interfacing.

Pin the interfacing into place on the bra cup.

Whipstitch the dart closed, working from the apex to the underwire.

Use a widely-spaced whipstitch and work your way around the bra. Knot the thread whenever you turn a corner, especially at the straps, center front, and where the bra band meets the cups.

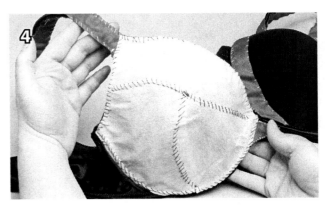

If you are planning on adding heavy design elements, reinforce the area you plan on stitching your surface embellishments on with additional stitching. Use a whipstitch or backstitch.

Cover the Center Front

The first piece that gets stitched to your bra is the center front. This piece gets put on first because the bra cups overlap this piece. This piece is small and can be tricky to handle, but be patient and use lots of pins. This piece is small enough that if you accidentally clip too deeply, you probably will have a scrap left over to cut a new one.

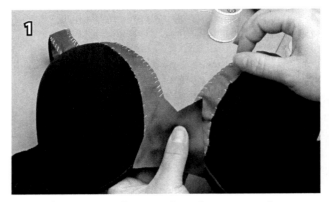

Center the piece over the center front. Leave an equal amount of seam allowance at top and bottom.

Clip into the seam allowance of the top and bottom of the piece almost to the fold line. You may need to clip quite a few times to accommodate a very tight curve.

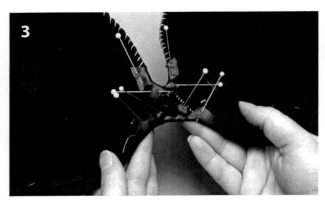

When you are done cutting and pinning, your piece should resemble the photo above.

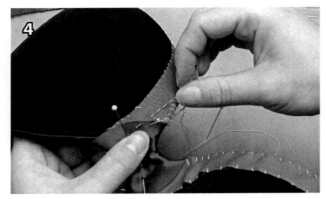

Use a smooth, even whipstitch around the entire center piece. When you approach a corner, make a knot before doing the next side.

The finished center front panel should look approximately like this.

If you have a decorative surface embellishment that will completely cover the grosgrain ribbon, you can skip this step and just stitch your surface decoration directly to strap. However, if you want your strap to perfectly match your cups and band, these methods will completely coordinate the finished garment.

You may want to try your bra on one last time to make sure your bra straps are perfectly adjusted. Now is the time to make any adjustments before you cover them.

Method One

If your covering fabric is scratchy, apply it only to the top of the grosgrain. In this method, your fabric is treated like a decorative ribbon that is slightly wider than the grosgrain so it doesn't show.

Method Two

If your covering fabric is smooth or soft, wrapping the entire strap completely encases the grosgrain ribbon, making the grosgrain completely disappear. If you tuck things into your costume, such as veils or cash, this method means that if the strap rolls or the inside inadvertently whips into view, the audience sees nothing.

Method One – Fold your seam allowances under and press with an iron. If the fabric is too delicate to press, then fold and use pins to hold in place.

Pin this strip of fabric to the outside of the bra strap. This view from underneath illustrates how the outer fabric needs to extend beyond the grosgrain to obscure it from view.

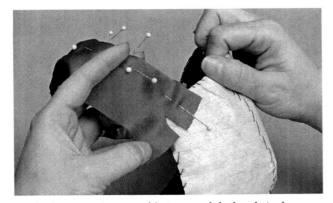

Method Two – Wrap your fabric around the band. At the cup and band, snip to release, allowing the fabric to wrap around the front and back of the band without bulging.

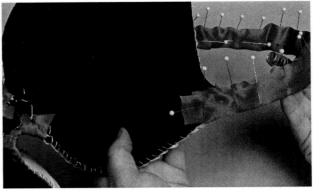

Fold one edge under and pin into place. The result should look like the image above. Slip stitch the folded edge. Whipstitch the raw edges on the cup and band ends.

Cover the Band

While draping the bra cup pattern was the most complex part of Phase II, in the this phase covering the bra band is the most tricky step. Why? Well, in many cases you will be sewing a woven, non-stretching fabric to a garment designed to stretch and yet provide firm support. Most bra bands are composed of many different pieces of elastic and stretch fabric so they stretch different directions and amounts. The band needs to remain stretchy to comfortably fit your body.

The other feature that further complicates this project is the hook end. You need to balance the needs of completely encasing your bra with fabric and hiding the original fabric, yet you want to keep those hooks free so you can use them to open and close your bra.

Some dancers swap out the stretchy flexible band for a sturdy, unyielding band, but this is a lot of work and is not as comfortable. Instead, for beginners I recommend using the band that's already there and simply encasing it with the same fabric as the rest of the bra. That way, you are not altering the structure of the bra. Even if your first bra project isn't sewn with neatness and precision, at least it will have a functional structure. Any cosmetic mistakes can be fixed without risking the integrity of the garment.

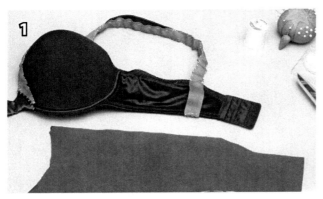

Baste the lining and outside fabric together along the bottom edge. This is just to hold these pieces together as you work with them. You will be sewing them more permanently as part of the final steps.

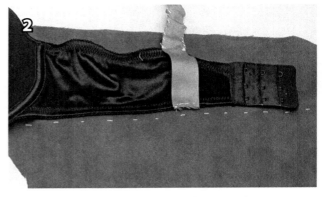

Open these pieces so that the seam allowance is facing up. Lay the bra in place, aligning the bottom edge with the basted seam and the edge of the cup. Pin the fabric to the cup.

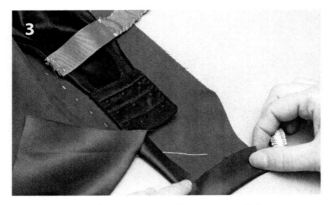

At the hook end, fold your seam allowance up all the way around on the outside fabric. You may want to lightly press this area with a cool iron. There are two sides to the hook and eye closure. On one side it will show and on the other it will be against the skin. On the side that shows, be sure to fold neatly.

Pull the hook end into position onto the folded-and-pinned fabric. Carefully adjust the folds at this point to make sure that the entire end is obscured from the outside.

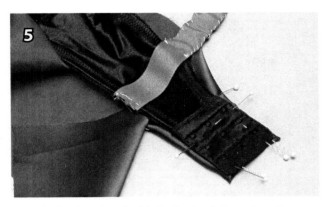

Baste the hook end to the fabric. Basting helps reduce the number of pins you will have to deal with in the next set of steps.

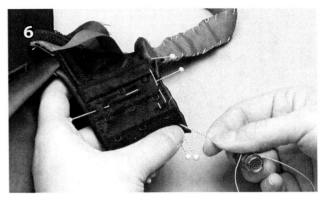

I am using white thread in this photo so you can see what is happening. You may want your basting stitches to match your fabric so you don't have to pull them out when you are finished.

Fold up the other side of the fabric and smooth into place. To allow the hooks to be accessible, the excess fabric needs to be trimmed.

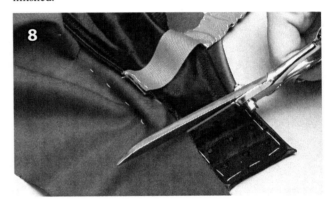

Leave enough fabric to turn the raw end under for a smooth finish.

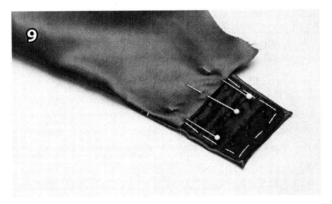

Fold the seam allowance under, keeping it neat and smooth. Pin into place. The next step, not shown, is to begin folding the upper edge under.

When sitched, the result should look like this. When you are finished, remove the basting sitches.

Cover the Band

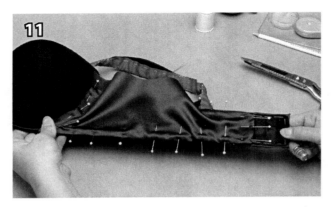

Fold the fabric up at the cup end and pin into place. To evenly distribute the extra fabric needed to accommodate the stretch, pull gently on the strap. Place pins every inch or so.

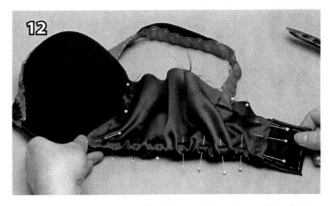

When you release tension, the fabric will bunch up. This fabric should be evenly distributed between the pins. If there are any larger bulges, release the pins, stretch the band, and re-pin. This may take a few tries.

Fold the upper seam allowance under along one side, pinning it to the band. Repeat on the other side. Again, you want to pull the band and pin the fabric to it evenly. If you see any large bulges, unpin and try again. This takes a lot of fiddling about.

Test to see if the band cover is smooth when stretched.

Slip stitch around the entire bra strap. You will be stitching the front cover to the back cover. Avoid catching the stretching band inside. Whipstitch the raw end to the bra cup.

When you get to the embellishment phase, remember to take into consideration the back of your bra. Many dancers forget that the audience will get a 360° view. Plan on taking your surface embellishment scheme all the way around the bra.

If your hair is long or if youl be wearing other costume pieces such as a cropped vest or cape, you may want to leave your bra band unembellished. Or you can use a luxurious fabric that is visually dynamic on its own.

When you sew on your surface embellishments, keep in mind that the bra band stretches. Use individual stitches, knot frequently, and cut the stitches apart. You may want to tack elements on rather than sew all the way around edges. Try on your bra and place your embellishments when fully stretched. If you simply sew them on without allowing for stretch, the bra will pull—or worse, not fit.

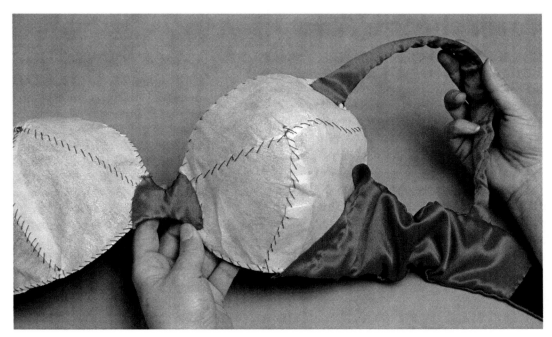

Stop and take a moment to inspect your work. At this point you should have the bra reinforced with grosgrain and covered with interfacing. The center front, strap, and bands should be covered with the outside fabric. Make sure to do this on both sides, bringing the entire bra to the same level of completion. Try on the bra. Make sure that the band fits and lies smoothly around your body and that the covers of the straps have no drag lines. This is the time to fix any problems.

Before you begin covering the bra cups, trim away any long threads. Test your stitching to make sure that your work is sturdy and ready for the next construction steps. This is a great time to further reinforce your bra along lines of stress. If you plan on having multiple rows of heavy decoration, you may want to add additional rows to your stitching.

The outside should resemble the image above; the inside should look like the photo below.

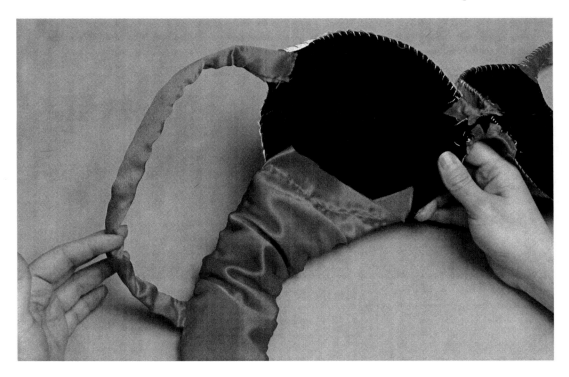

Cover the Bra Cups

You will see some similarities between these photos and the images on pages 27–31, when you draped your bra cover. However, during this phase you will use the pattern that is pre-cut and shaped to fit your bra. While working through this phase, you may want to pin both cups together and into place to make sure your darts are aligned.

When you begin sewing your bra, work in a circle. Beginning at the center of the cup, stitch your dart down first. Make sure that when you are stitching that you go through the bra cup. This will keep it from shifting when you are sewing other parts of the bra.

A word of caution when working with knits

Many dancers like to use stretch fabrics in their costumes for comfort and movement. If you are covering your bra in stretchy fabric, take extra care. If you tug, stretch, or pull the fabric, you can inadvertently distort the shape of the bra. If you are using stretch fabric, carefully inspect your cup before you begin sewing. If you see any drag lines or if you feel the foam of the cup rippling or buckling from below, pull out the pins and start again. This is a very easy mistake to make when working with knits but being aware will help you get the best results possible.

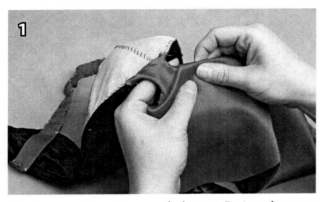

Center your pattern piece over the bra cup. Begin at the center at the top of the band. Fold the fabric over the upper edge of the cup all the way to the strap. Pin into place.

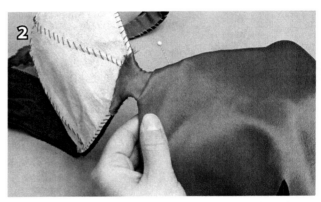

Gently fold the seam allowance under at the edge where the cup meets the center front. This area may be visible to the audience when you are finished, so fold neatly.

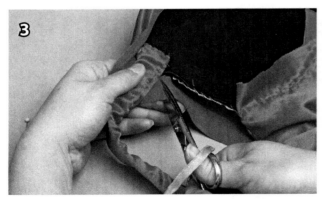

Turn the bra over so you can see the inside. At the strap, clip the fabric almost to the point where the strap and the bra cup meet.

Turn the bra back over. Neatly fold the tab under in front of the strap. If you need to clip a little deeper to get it to fold and lay smoothly, be careful. Pin into place.

Flip the bra over. Continue working around the bra. Clip notches into the seam allowance at the side of the bra between the strap and the band.

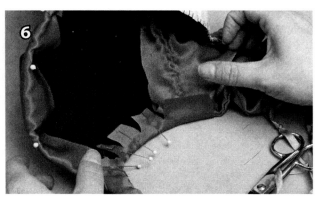

Fold the seam allowance up and pin. Notice how the notches have spread release the tension.

Flip the bra back over so you are looking at the outside. Smooth your fingers over the bra to make sure that everything is in position. Then fold the seam allowance under at the bra band.

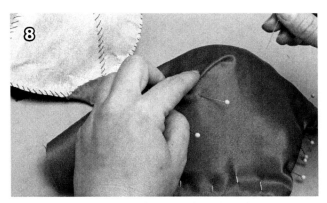

Smooth the fabric inwards from all of the pinned seams. As you gently work the fabric towards the dart, you may want to place some pins in the fabric to hold it still. At the apex of the bust, begin the top fold of the dart.

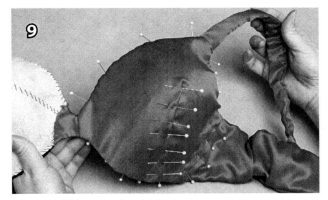

Continue folding the dart under, working your way to the lower edge of the cup. Pin as necessary. Hold your bra up and take a look at it. If you see any draglines or puckers, release the pins in that area, smooth, and try again.

When ready for sewing, the bra should resemble the photos here and in step 9. Use sturdy thread and a closely spaced whipstitch around all of the raw edges on the inside of the bra. Use a slip stitch to sew the dart around the bra band and strap.

Add Padding

Most dancers have toyed with the idea of enhancing their bounty with additional padding. Some bra styles allow the dancer to increase her perceived bust size by as much as two full cups. While it is impossible to transform an A-cup beauty into a busty C-cup, adding a little padding can help create the illusion of volume.

But padding is not just for smaller builds. Bust pads can help put your cleavage where you want it by serving as a "shelf." When pads are added, they change the fit of the cup and reshape the upper cleavage line. Performers with uneven or lopsided breasts can use padding to even out the shape and size of their bust. Make sure to fit your bra to the larger breast size, then pad the smaller side up from the bottom.

If you know you like to pad your bra, plan ahead and shop accordingly. Buy a cup size bigger than you generally wear with the knowledge that you will be padding to fit. Larger cups give the viewer the perception of bigger breasts, regardless of what's inside of your bra. No matter what effect you are shooting for, it is best to give your padding a test before stitching it in and then lining the bra. Make sure to put the bra on and play with the positioning, size, and shape of your pads. When it's right, it will show in the mirror.

Plunge or push-up bra – For dancers seeking that "kissing cleavage" look, pads will push the breasts together. Locate the pads on the lower outer edges by putting one corner at the center front and the other at the middle of the band or side.

Strapless or convertible bra – For this style, the goal is to lift the breasts up as two individual mounds. Place the pad at the bottom center of the cup to form a shelf upon which to lay the breasts.

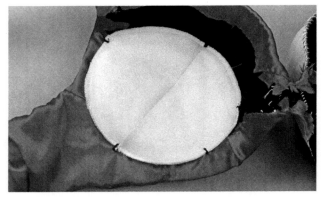

Stitch the pads – Some dancers merely pin their pads in for easy removal, but pins can come loose. Ouch! Prevent pain with a simple catch-stitch of four or five loops at each end. This will hold the pad in place, yet still be easy to snip and remove if necessary. Firmly stitched pads will not pop out.

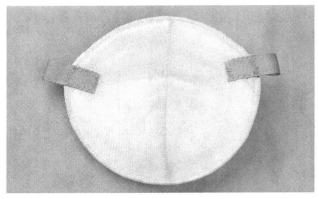

If you have only one set of pads, you can sew tabs onto them to use as an anchor for safety pins. Alternatively, you can use snaps to hold your pads in, yet allow for quick removal.

Line the Bra

One of the most frequently skipped steps in the bra making process is lining the bra. Lining gives the bra a good finish, making it look as good inside as out. The lining serves several important functions in the finished bra and is an essential element to include if you are a professional seamstress who is designing and making embellished bras for clients.

Lining the bra makes cleaning easy. If you plan on wearing a bra many times, the lining will lie against the skin and absorb perspiration. Linings can be changed to instantly freshen a bra. If you ever plan on selling your embellished bra, you can swap out the tired lining for fresh, clean fabric.

Depending on what kind of thread has been used to stitch on the embellishments, the inside of the bra might be scratchy, lumpy, or uncomfortable. Alternately, if you use padding to add shape to the cleavage or enhance the bustline, then a lining will hide the presence of padding.

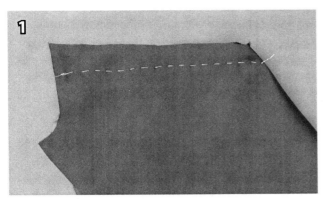

Using your bra cup cover pattern, cut out two pieces of your lining fabric. Hand or machine stitch the dart into place. If you are hand-stitching the dart, use a simple, even baste with your stitches closely placed for strength.

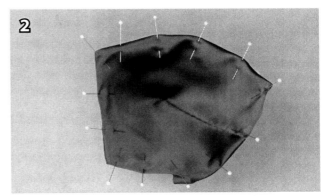

Using an iron, press the seam allowance under, folding it 1/4" smaller. Press all edges under on both lining pieces. This view is looking straight down into the cup.

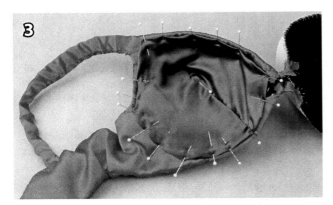

Place the stitched and pressed lining into the bra cup. Pin into place, making sure that your lining is folded under enough not to show from the outside.

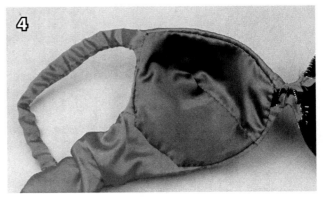

Slip stitch the lining into the cup, working the cup in this order. Upper edge first, center front, lower edge, then side last. If the lining seems too loose, you can make an anchor stitch through the lining into the inside of the cup at the apex.

Phase IV – Embellishments

A bra without embellishment is like a cake without frosting. Choosing embellishments that fit your dance style, your personality, and your budget can be tricky but the rewards are great. You can make a plain bra look expensive and exotic without depleting your budget.

Well-placed fringe enhances both your figure and your dance moves. Beading and appliqués add sparkle and shine. Tribal jewelry provides a hint of the exotic along with an echo of the rich ancestral culture of the dance. Coins add weight and sound while ribbons and braid make even a plain fabric look rich and textured.

With a little planning, the embellishment phase can be a fun and creative way to add individual personality to your overall design. Read through the embellishment section and look at the examples of design elements presented. Keep your mind open and think about how you can combine these different elements within your design.

Below – Bra encased in beaded appliqués with rows of designer fringe.

There are an infinite number of embellishment styles and techniques to choose from. In the course of a two-hour workshop or a small book like this one, we cannot even begin to scratch the surface. The possibilities are endless and restricted only by availability and budget.

Establish your budget

The embellishment phase can cost more than all the other phases combined. In fact, I have known dancers who have spent hundreds of dollars just to embellish a single bra! Before you spend any money on materials, plan your design and figure out what your budget will be. Consider your entire costume. Will you be making a matching belt, skirt, or dress?

Inexpensive options

Ribbon and chainette fringe – Available at most local fabric stores, this is probably the least expensive decorating option.

Coins – A row or two of decorative coins can enhance a bra without breaking the bank. And coins look really good when layered over chainette fringe.

Recycle embellished fabrics – Some dancers hunt the resale shops looking for beaded or sequined garments to recycle into costume pieces. This is a great way of saving money, saving the environment, and (depending on the thrift store) contributing to a charitable organization all at the same time.

Mid-priced options

Beaded appliqués with chainette fringe – To add a little bit of shine, excitement, and flash to the fringe, stitch on a few paillettes.

Hand beading the surface of the bra – This is very time-consuming but can save a lot of cash. Custom beaded fringe and swags bring shine, pattern, and excitement to your costume. If you do the work, you save the cash.

Costume jewelry – One of the fastest ways of embellishing a bra is to use jewelry pieces. They go on in a snap and look fabulous. Good-looking costume or tribal jewelry can get pricey but if you shop wisely or use vintage or recycled pieces you can help keep the cost low.

Expensive options

Use fabulous beaded fabrics – One of the quickest ways to increase the cost of your project is to use pre-beaded fabrics. Jewel-encrusted materials can get quite expensive but save a lot of time because you only have to sew on one piece of cloth, not each individual jewel.

Encrust your bra with rhinestones and crystal – If money is no object, use only the finest materials and enjoy the glamour and luxury that only the finest can offer.

Hire someone else to do the work! If you like to design your own costumes but have more cash than time, why not hire a seamstress to bring your original designs to life?

Embellishment

Once you have settled on a budget, style, and a look that you are trying to achieve, now is the time to plan exactly how you will reach your goals.

Use your bra cup pattern to plan your design

We've already used the pattern you made for the bra cup to cover the base lingerie bra. Now we will use this same pattern piece to plan out the design. Using your cup pattern to practice layout and design allows you to really think through your embellishments without having to waste excessive time basting, sewing, or undoing a mistake.

Before you go further, you may want to cut out a second bra cup pattern so that you can "test drive" the look of your full design. Use a pencil to draw on your pattern what you want to include on your bra and where you want to put it.

If you plan on doing a lot of hand beading on your bra, take your pattern down to your local bead shop and plot some layouts. Many bead shops provide tables where you can work out your designs. Alternatively, you can lay your pattern in a flat tray and lay your beads out accordingly.

For designs that involve a lot of linear elements like braid, ribbon, and trims, take the pattern with you to your local fabric store and check out the assortment of designs that are available. Play with the trim. Lay it on the pattern piece to get an idea of how the width relates to the shape and size of the cup. Some dancers even color their pattern piece with pencils or markers to get a better idea of how the final garment will look.

Don't be afraid to just whip out your pattern piece in a store. If you are shopping for appliqués in person, ask to see one so you can lay it directly on your pattern. For Internet shopping, make sure to get the dimensions and roughly sketch in light pencil on your pattern. If the design works for you, then go for it and buy the appliqués. Otherwise, simply erase the design and try again.

Two Ways to Add Beads and Shine

Above – a bra is encrusted with four large floral appliqués with a double row of designer fringe. This is a low-time/high-cost alternative.

Below – a bra has been hand-beaded with a geometric design and custom-beaded swags. This is a time-consuming—but low-budget—option.

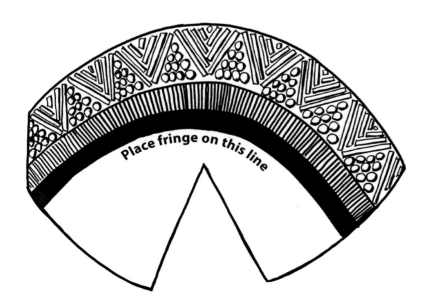

Place fringe on this line

Fringe – What It Can Do for *You!*

Above – In this detail, a single row of contrasting fringe is placed horizontally accross the apex of the bust. Notice how it hangs freely below the bust.

Below – Many rows of beaded designer fringe are built up from the bottom edge of the cups. The rows end in a vertical line that cuts across the bust apex. The rows of fringe create a stunning visual texture and a tremendous amount of movment.

Fringe accentuates your motions, amplifying their size, shape, and direction. Fringe makes it possible for someone in the back of the room to see even subtle movements. Styles in fringe, like all aspects of fashion, change with taste. For many dancers, the choice of fringe—because of the expense to purchase or the time required to build it—determines the style, shape, and decoration of the finished bra.

Fringe placement should be determined not only by the style of the bra but also by your personal dance vocabulary. Since you are designing your own costume, the fringe can be placed to best accentuate your performance style.

Do a lot of shimmies? Use short densely packed fringe. The short length allows the fringe to fly and densely packing the fringe creates a full, thick spray.

Use twisting movements? Longer fringe whips about and accentuate twists.

Swaying motions? Place fringe on the sides of the costumes. Swaying motions are accentuated by the flip of long fringe suspended from the chest and hip.

You should also consider your own body style and shape when designing with fringe.

Short torso? Keep fringe short on the bra to visually lengthen your torso.

Want to look taller? A V-shape draws visual lines that accentuate height.

Want to look leaner? Place the bulk of your fringe at the center front to draw the eye in.

Fringe alternatives are quite popular and offer dancers a wide variety of design options.

Coins are perhaps the most traditional and frequently used alternative to fringe for decorating dance costumes. They can be authentic coins that have been punched or drilled for use. Pressed coins ranging from tiny, light, and inexpensive to more pricey styles made from heavier metals are available from dance suppliers.

Necklaces with dangling elements can be stitched onto the surface of the bra to create movement and shine. Look for necklaces that you can build onto an entire costume piece. Remember that when you are using jewelry you will need to match the design elements on your belt.

Jewelry components in various forms can be used in clusters, arranged in rows or combined with coins or chainette fringe to add a layer of sparkle and shine. These can be purchased new from bead shops. Older jewelry pieces can be harvested, disassembled, and the parts used. This is a great way to recycle older costume jewelry pieces.

Fringe Styles

Most dancers use some sort of decorative fringe or dangling decorative elements. When you are contemplating the type of fringe to use on a costume, consider its expense, your sewing skills, and the amount of time you have available to work on the garment.

Ready-made fringe is good for first-time seamstresses who are getting used to needlework and construction techniques. It saves time and is easy to install. Ready-made fringe can be further customized and embellished by adding paillettes, additional charms, or decorative needlework.

Egyptian fringe, which is designed and made for the belly dance community, is a sturdy beaded fringe made from seed beads or rocailles, occasionally with larger accent beads and paillettes as accents.

Designer fringe is available through fabric stores and is used by crafters and fashion and interior designers. This fringe is more widely spaced and mounted on a ribbon or cord. The beads are usually plastic, although glass is sometimes used on more upscale versions.

Chainette fringe is a great alternative to beaded styles. Made from looped rayon, chainette is available in a wide variety of colors, is easy to dye, and comes in a variety of common lengths. This style of fringe is great for beginner costumes, historical, tribal, and Gypsy styles.

Hand beading is the best way to get a truly customized look for your costume. You can build your fringe directly onto the surface of the bra. This requires stitching through the padding and reinforcement and makes a good, solid support. This technique gives the most custom look and the greatest amount of freedom with strand placement. Instead of a simple row, beaded fringe can be applied in clusters or at random over the surface of the bra.

You can build your fringe on a ribbon or band. If you build your fringe on a band, you can play with positioning, move to another bra if your size or shape changes, or if the bra wears out from use. However, you need to plan your design to conceal the ribbon or create a decorative embellishment to cover it.

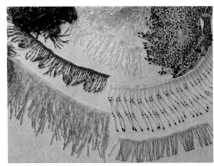

Above – Examples of Egyptian fringe.
Middle – Assortment of designer fringe.
Below – Bra with tassles & beaded fringe.

Below – Examples of textile-based fringes. These styles of fringe are available in most fabric stores. Check in the upholstery sections for tassle fringe.

Left – Chainette fringe. **Center** – Tassel fringe. **Right** – Beaded tassel fringe.

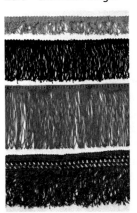

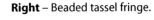

Fringe Placement

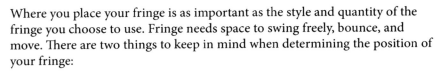

Where you place your fringe is as important as the style and quantity of the fringe you choose to use. Fringe needs space to swing freely, bounce, and move. There are two things to keep in mind when determining the position of your fringe:

Place your fringe at the apex of your bust for maximum swing and movement. This allows your fringe to flow, bounce, and swing the most. Many dancers apply multiple rows of fringe to their costume and, if this is part of your design plan, you may want to place the uppermost row of fringe right across the apex of your bust.

Fringe needs to be able to move. Resist the urge to put the fringe at the tops of your bra cups. Fringe needs to be freely suspended or, at the very least, mounted so it lays across a vertical part of the body. If your fringe is mounted above the apex of the bust, it might "split," parting and hanging down either side of the bust mound.

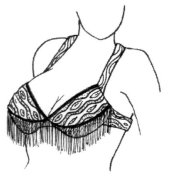

If you are going for a 1920s flapper look or have a small cup size, you may be able to get away with putting fringe higher on the bra. If you decide to do this, make sure that the fringe matches the fabric underneath so if it "splits" over the bust it won't be so obvious. Alternatively, you may want to emphasize this effect with high contrast materials. It's your choice as designer.

Preparing and applying fringe

Fringe takes a lot of stress. Centrifugal forces are stronger at the ends of the fringe. When you are putting the fringe onto your costume, apply it with sturdy, closely-spaced stitches and knot the thread frequently.

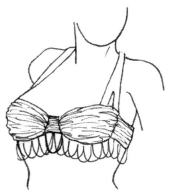

Pre-prepare your fringe. Using an adhesive product to seal down the knots before you sew it to your garment will extend the life of your fringe. Glue along the top of the fringe. If you are using beaded fringe, put a dollop of glue at the tips as well.

Use heavy-duty thread. I suggest carpet-weight or upholstery-weight thread in nylon or cotton-covered polyester for this use. Fringe can be quite heavy, especially the beaded varieties, so use the strongest thread you can find.

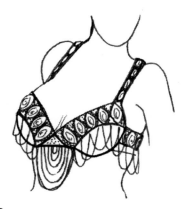

Examples of Fringe Placement

An assortment of sketches demonstrating popular fringe positions. Notice how all of these deisngs position the fringe below the apex of the bust.

This is also a demonstration of how the croquis on page 11 can be used as a design tool to play with the surface embellishments of your bra.

Ribbons, Braid, and Strings of Sequins

Linear design elements are a great resource for the dance costume designer. Although they all look different and produce different design effects, linear elements are great for directing the eye of the viewer. Each of these elements can be used individually or built up into complex groups to give a lush, rich appearance.

Braids, ribbons, and other trims can easily be stitched on using a slip stitch. Simply lay the braid where you want it on the bra, pin it into place, and then sew. Some designers like to pin both cups, carefully try the bra on, and compare. If you are following the upper cup edge, your design will automatically line up. Test horizontally-placed trim. Pinning both sides and comparing can help prevent disaster and a lot of re-sewing.

Styles of trim

Rhinestones and appliqués – For dancers interested in the ultimate glitz and glamour, yet wanting the speed of sewing simple lines, strings of rhinestones and small appliqués fit the bill. Although the appliqués can be cut apart and used as individual motifs, these strings of appliqués can be quickly stitched onto bras with a quick and easy whipstitch or permanent baste. See (A) below.

Sequins on strings – Sewing individual sequins is a time-consuming process. Using sequined fabric is a quick and fast, but expensive, alternative. In between there is a middle ground: sequins on strings. The nice part of sequins on strings is that they are very flexible. They can be used to make straight lines or trace fluid curves. Simply whipstitch them into place, hiding the stitches in the overlapping sequins. See (B) below.

Ribbons – Ribbons can add historic or ethnic flare to a costume. Wide, ornate ribbons can add flash and shine when metallic threads are woven into their complex patterns. Ribbons work well when presented layered and combined. Some designers save money by using several narrower and inexpensive ribbons to build up a more impressive design treatment. See (C) below.

Gimp and braid – A wide variety of braided trims are available in fabric stores in both the dress trims and upholstery areas. Gimp is a three-dimensional braid that can be used to add not only color but texture to the embellishment of your bra. See (D) below.

Use a variety of narrower braids to build up to a rich finish. In this example, we have used four different linear design elements to create a rich wide band full of texture. We chose two colors, black and gold, and selected a group of coordinating trim. The final result appears on the bra at the top of page 56. At bottom, a bra in progress with three rows of braid at the upper cups as the first layer of embellishement.

Appliqués

Appliqués are one of the most versatile and easy ways to integrate a lot of shine and sparkle into the design of your embellished bra. While you can almost always find "wedding white" appliqués in standard fabric stores, bright or unique colors can be tricky to locate. Look for specialty vendors in your area and on the Internet to find the styles and colors you need to complete your design. Many dancers use appliqués because of these major benefits:

Saves time. Appliqués can be expensive, but they replace both your time and the costs of the beads, sequins, and other embellishment items. Using pre-made appliqués saves time because you can very quickly stitch on appliqués, while the alternative, sewing sequins or beads by hand, can be quite time-consuming.

Easy to attach. A simple whipstitch, back stitch, or even a sturdy small basting stitch quickly and easily attaches the appliqué to the bra. You won't need to learn complex beading stitches nor will you need the special needles and thread that beading requires.

They can be recycled. When you purchase a set of appliqués to use on your ensemble, you are not committed to using them only on that one costume. If you tire of the overall look, if your size changes, or if the costume becomes damaged, you can remove the appliqués and transfer them to another gament. With surface beading, you have fewer options for moving your beading intact.

You can customize. Make a store-bought appliqué your own by adding more beads and embellishments to it. Gluing on a few rhinestones, stitching on contrasting beads, or building up more design can punch up an appliqué.

Top left – A combination of appliqués, braid, and gems.
Center left – Large appliqué with rhinestones.
Bottom left – Bra with clustered appliqués.
Below – Assorted appliqués.

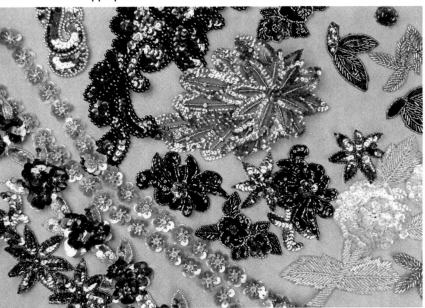

Surface Beading

Beading isn't difficult, but it is quite time-consuming. This painstaking work is well worth the effort, for it produces the ultimate in custom-designed glamour. There are many approaches to beading techniques. At its most basic, beading involves stitching each bead onto the cloth. Remember to knot your thread frequently. Some beaders knot between each individual bead.

Adhesive products are essential for extending the life of your beaded work. Go over the back side of your completed design and dab on some glue to really nail down your work and prevent it from unraveling. For flat-backed gems and rhinestones, sturdy glue is essential. Make sure the glue you select dries clear, adheres to a variety of materials, and has some give. Test your glue on a scrap of fabric with your design elements to ensure that the fabric and stones will not discolor.

Plan your design. Use your bra cup pattern piece to draw or trace a custom design. You can use this as a template and literally place your beads on the pattern piece to test your design. Take your pattern to your favorite bead shop. Practice with the beads they have available by laying them out on your sketched design.

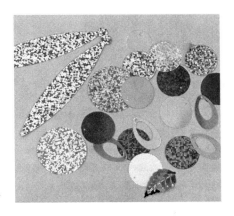

Always buy extra beads. It is far better to have too many than too few and have to try to match a dye-lot. Having extra beads allows you to perform repairs or alterations on your costume in the future.

Use beaded fabric. The fastest way to bead the surface of your garment is to buy pre-sequined or pre-beaded fabric. Use your pattern to position the design perfectly on the bra. Before you trace and cut the design, take the time to glue down any loose threads and dab glue onto any knots.

Bead a pattern. One of the quickest ways to bead is to follow a pattern in woven or printed fabric, ribbon, or trim. Select a element of the design to highlight and then repeat the process throughout the design.

Use clip art. There are many clip art books available in bookstores, craft shops, and fine art stores. Look at a few of these clip art resources. These books are filled with floral or geometric patterns that can be interpreted in beads. You may want to check out the embroidery design section of your local craft store for even more ideas.

Below left – An assortment of beads.

Below right – An assortment of stones.

Top right – Bra with geometric beading.

Middle right – An assortment of paillettes.

Bottom right – Bra with scatterbeading.

Coins and Chain

Coins

One of the oldest and most enduring clothing embellishments is the stitching of coins, items for barter, and valuable trinkets to the surface of clothing. Historically, nomadic peoples have stitched their wealth into their clothing for portability and accessibility. Many performers at historical venues, re-enactors, and neo-tribalists use this traditional use of coinage to create costumes that harken back to days of old. Belly dancers who favor a Gypsy, historical, or tribal look continue to sew both real and imitation coins onto their costumes.

Real coins – Coins are quite heavy but this is offset by the warm rich sound they generate when they clink together. Coins from around the world that are no longer in current use are available from coin shops and through specialty vendors. While many coin styles already have holes in them, most need to be either drilled or punched.

Pressed coins – Imitation coins made from pressed aluminum, brass, or tin are much lighter and come with a hole to stitch onto clothes. However, these faux coins produce a very high-pitched or faint noise when they hit each other. Costumes made with imitation coins are lighter weight and need less structural support to maintain their shape. And they are a good choice for dancers who are quite acrobatic.

Specialty coins – Saroyan Zills carries a line of mid-weight forged coins that produce a clean, clear, sparkling ring during movement. These coins are made with dancers in mind and produce melodic tones. Contact information for Saroyan is available in the resources directory on page 62.

Above – Saroyan coins sound as good as they look on this coin bra with braid trim.
Middle – An assortment of pressed coins.
Below – Coin and chain bra cover, courtesy of Aunty Magpie's Shining Hoard

Chains

For a completely metallic look, chains can be used to add swags and drops instead of other types of fringe. Chain is available in a wide variety of metals to coordinate with all of the most popular coin types including gold, copper, brass and silver. Inexpensive brass/gold and silver-colored chain can be purchased at most hardware stores. Use sturdy thread to whipstitch onto the bra.

Coins and chains work well together. Adding coins to chain is a simple process that requires only a pair of jewelry or needle-nosed pliers and jump rings. Jump rings are little metal circles that are used to hold metal jewelry components together. These can be found in many bead stores and craft shops. If this sounds like a fun way to make a costume, you may want to visit your local bead store for a quick demonstration on how to effectively use jump rings. Prevent jump rings from coming loose by using a drop of strong glue.

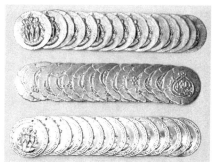

Tribal Jewelry

Tribal jewelry is a broad term that describes traditional, ethnic, and vintage jewelry styles from around the world. From Morocco to India, and China to Africa, there is a vast array of styles of jewelry that fall under this umbrella. This style of jewelry can instantly give a bra a lot of drama and punch. With the global influences that are happening in clothing today, incorporating multicultural design elements into an ensemble can really give your costume a unique look, no matter what style of dancing you do.

Sewing the jewelry on can be a bit tricky. Locate the place on the jewelry piece where the object is the strongest. Loops, hooks, and bars where jewelry is designed to interconnect are perfect places to stitch the piece into place. Use heavy-duty upholstery thread to bar-tack the pieces on. It is best to reinforce your bra with a heavy-duty interfacing prior to covering to help support and distribute the weight of heavy jewelry.

India – Bright shimmering gold and silver jewelry, delicate and light, can bring the glamour and excitement of "Bollywood" to your costumes. Look for matched pairs of anklets to place on the upper edge of each bra cup. A delicate nose ring or elegant brooch placed at the center front of the costume can finish the effect.

Africa – Look for cowry shells and necklaces made of semi-precious stone beads, bone, and other natural materials. One approach is to pick a geographic or cultural region, then select key colors and motifs to use throughout your costume.

Middle East – For tribal-style belly dancers, there is a tremendous amount of jewelry to choose from. From Western India to Turkey, Egypt, and beyond, this region has a rich tradition of jewelry display and personal adornment. The image at bottom right illustrates how a collection of pieces from different regions has been tied together, through repeated shapes, color of metal, and the lapis paste to create a collage of jewelry pieces that looks dynamite as a finished bra.

Top – Detail of tribal bra.
Above – Stones, shells, and amber.
Below – Tribal bra with Kutchi jewelry.
Below left – Tribal jewelry assortment.

Other regions – Feel free to explore other options. If you are making an embellished bra to perform to a particular piece of ethnic music or to evoke a specific locale, look at the jewelry traditions from the region and see if you can pull from their elements to decorate your bra.

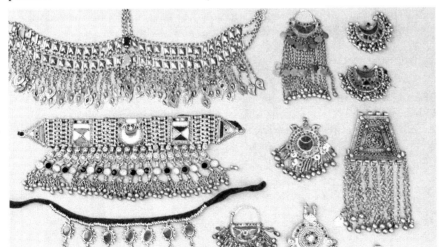

Hand Sewing Techniques

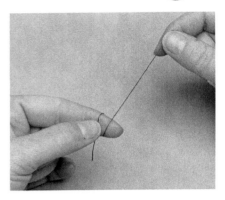

Thread selection

A standard cotton-covered polyester thread is easy to use, comes in a variety of colors, and is quite strong. Rayon thread is less strong and is good for attaching lightweight embellishments. Silk thread is strong, has a beautiful luster, and is great for hand sewing, but it can be more difficult to find and more expensive.

When attaching heavy decorative embellishments, such as jewelry pieces, chain, or coins, you need a stronger thread. Button and carpet twist is a strong cotton thread that is thicker than standard thread, but still easy to use. Upholstery weight thread in nylon is sturdy and is easy to sew but is quite thick and requires needles with large eyes.

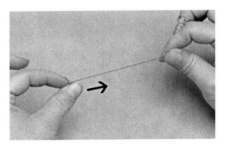

Thread color

Throughout this book, contrasting thread was used to allow the thread to show. When you are making your costume bra, make sure to match your thread in both color and tone. For instance, if you are covering a black bra with red fabric, use black thread and grosgrain ribbon to prepare the bra. Then switch to red when you stitch on the cover. If you are using contrasting colored trim, pick a thread that disappears into the color and texture of the trim. Many seamstresses keep a basic supply of colors including black, white, and gray. Dancers may want to invest in gold and silver as well.

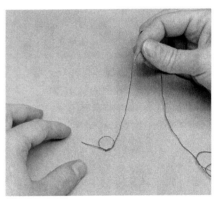

Knotting the thread

Many new seamstresses find this first step confusing and difficult. Before you sew, you need to put an anchoring knot at the end of the thread. The pictures at left show how to quickly place a knot in the thread.

Needles

Needle selection is highly personalized. Some seamstresses like small needles for maneuverability while others can get a better grip and more control on longer needles. The size of the eye can play a role in selection. Larger eyes are easier to thread but are wider and thicker and can be more difficult to pass through finely woven fabrics. If you don't already have a needle preference and have never used different styles of needles such as sharps, betweens, millinery, and so forth, buy an assortment of needles and experiment with them until you find a size and shape that fits your hand and sewing style.

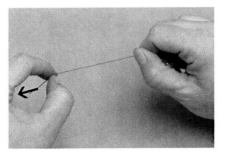

Beading needles

To sew beads with small holes, such as bugles and small seed beads, special beading needles are must. These long and very slender needles are designed to pass through even the tiniest holes, making them very difficult to thread. As you sew with beading needles, they will begin to curve in your hand and if you use too much force they can snap.

Wrap the thread once around your index finger. Rub the thread between your finger and thumb. This will loop the thread around itself. Then just tug to cinch the knot. Easy!

There are four main stitches used in this book. Each stitch has its own unique properties. If you are an experienced sewer, you may have your own arsenal of stitches that will work perfectly for this project. Consider this list of suggestions. For a more complete list of stitches with step-by-step directions for making each stitch, consult a good general sewing book such as the *New Complete Guide to Sewing*. For more information on this and other reference books, see page 63.

Helpful Hint

Beeswax can make thread that is unruly and prone to twisting better behaved to prevent knots and breakage. Apply the wax by drawing your thread across a cake of beeswax. This coats the thread, making it stiffer. If you can, iron the thread with a low setting to make the wax melt into the fibers to increase pliability, and make it easier to handle.

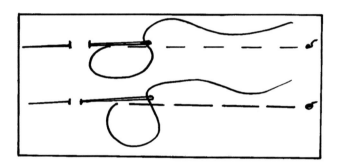

Basting – Basting is a fast stitch that is used to hold the layers together while you prepare for the more serious sewing. A long basting stitch makes a great marking tool if done in contrasting colors.

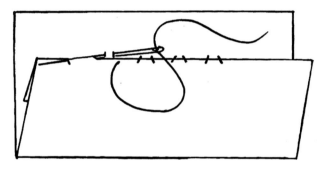

Slip stitch or blind hem – The slip stitch joins a folded edge to a flat piece of fabric. Used in bra making to sew the straps, apply trim, and neatly stitch in the lining.

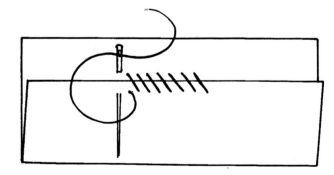

Whipstitch – The whipstitch is a quick stitch that is used to hold two pieces of cloth together. In our project, we use it to affix the bra covering fabric to the bra cup on the inside. This is a rather ugly stitch and should only be used in places that don't show.

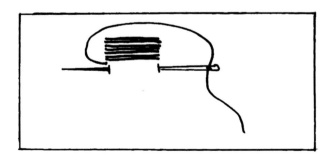

Tack – Used to reinforce areas of stress. Also used to stitch on the hooks and eyes and used to keep the bra straps from sliding.

Sewing Beads and Sequins

Single-bead stitch

The single-bead stitch is probably the most basic of beading techniques. The thread comes from the back of the cloth. A bead is slipped over the needle, slid down the thread, and seated against the cloth. A stitch is taken through the cloth to secure the bead, and the process continues. This is a very secure stitch, especially if a knot is tied between each bead. This stitch is used in scatter beading and in areas that require precise bead placement.

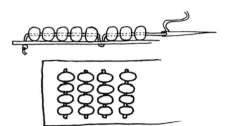

Lazy stitch

The lazy stitch covers a lot of territory more quickly than the single bead stitch. For this technique you may need a longer beading needle to stack up the beads. The beads are strung onto the thread, as many as eight seed beads can be applied in one stitch. Smooth the beads across the surface of the fabric, then take a stitch through the cloth and repeat. This technique can make straight lines or zigzag rows. This technique can also be worked as a fill stitch, working back and forth across the fabric rather than in a straight line.

Running stitch/back stitch

The backstitch is similar to the lazy stitch, except you use much shorter strands of beads, six or fewer. The row is laid across the fabric, making sure to control the tension so it's neither too tight nor too loose. When you take your next stitch through the cloth, go backwards and come back up between the last and second to the last bead. Loop back through the last bead. Continue forward with your next row. This is a very sturdy stitch, especially if you knot frequently.

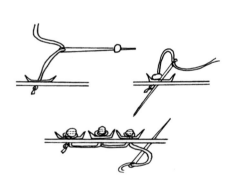

Sequins, flat technique

To apply a flat sequin, you can use one of two techniques. The most common is to use a seed bead to secure the sequin to the cloth. Pass a thread up through the fabric and string a sequin and one bead. Pass the needle back through the sequin, pulling the bead down to hold the sequin in place. If you choose not to use a bead, you can stitch across the sequin to hold it in place.

Sequins, layered technique

Begin by placing the first sequin on the cloth by passing a thread up through the center of the sequin and then stitching back through the fabric at the sequin's edge. Bring the thread up in the same location and place your sequin. Half of the first sequin, and the stitch used to hold it to the cloth, will be obscured by the second sequin. Repeat the stitch as needed.

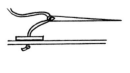  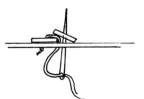 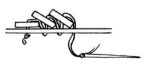

Care and Maintenance

Once your costume piece is complete, proper care and maintenance is vital to maintain its appearace and helps it last as long as possible.

Put together a repair kit. If you are building your own bra, be sure to construct a repair kit of beads, sequins, and other surface embellishments that match this costume. In the future, if you have to make routine repairs or alterations, you will have a supply of replacement parts and pieces at the ready.

Keep a tool box close by. If you keep a small box of essential sewing tools near your costume storage area, you are more likely to repair small problems before they become big ones.

Create a cleaning test sample. On a scrap of fabric, stitch a representative sample of the parts and pieces of your costume. Test wash your sample using more aggressive laundering techniques until you find the one that works most effectively. Water alone can damage some fibers, sequins, and beads, so be cautious and test carefully.

Conduct routine inspections. Look for loose fringe, dangling sequins, and other pieces that may be loose. Fix the damage before your next performance or it might dissappear in a whirl.

Lay your costume out to dry. Before storing your costume, make sure it is thoroughly dry to prevent mildew.

Store your costumes wisely. Don't hang costume pieces with dangling beads. Gravity will pull and weaken the threads. Store bras and belts flat in a box with adequate air circulation to prevent mildew. Including a desiccant such as silica gel to remove residual moisture and keep your garments fresh.

Change linings. When making your own costumes, make all linings removable. If you cannot wash your whole garment, simply change the linings to prevent perspiration from saturating the garment.

Remove perspiration scent. There are several ways to deodorize your costume. Store the costume with a fabric sack full of cornstarch to absorb scent. Use a commercial product, such as Febreeze®, to remove stubborn scents. Try an old theatre technique: lightly spritz a fine mist of 1 part vodka and 1 part water onto the linings of your garments. A traditional method is to hang your costume in a room with fragrant incense burning.

Rotate costumes. If you perform regularly and you don't have a uniform, you may want to alternate between costumes. Switching off between costumes extends the life of all the costumes you have in rotation. This also gives you ample time to allow each costume to thoroughly dry and to conduct routine maintenance and repairs.

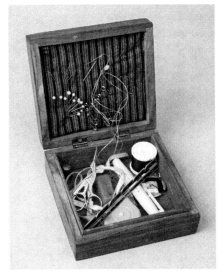

A small sewing kit.

A repair kit of beads, bugles, and sequins that match the costume below.

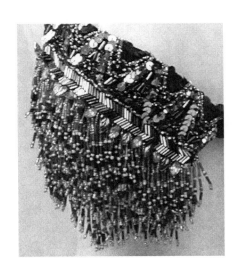

Resources

For more great resources for costume designers, read Davina's Blog.

www.davina.us

Here is a list of resources to help you in your search for information and supplies for constructing bras. List updated April 2011.

Bra-making Supplies on the Internet

Artemis Imports www.artemisimports.com
Dance vendor who carries unembellished cups

Bra-Makers Supply www.bramakers.com
Canadian dealer who carries all materials needed to build custom bras

General Bead www.genbead.com
Beads, rhinestones

Kwik-Sew® Patterns www.kwiksew.com
Several bra patterns that can be used to create custom bra cups

Laceland www.laceland.com
Bra-making patterns and supplies

Lace and Trim/Such a Deal www.laceandtrim.com
Ribbons, braids, chainette fringe and lace appliques

Realm of Regalia www.realmofregalia.com
Ribbon, trim, tribal jewelry, and other embellishments

Scheherezade Imports www.scheherezadeimports.com
Egyptian beads, costumes, and accessories

Sew Sassy Fabrics www.sewsassy.com
Bra-making supplies and patterns

Shipwreck Bead www.shipwreck.com
Beads, rhinestones

Sugar Petals www.sugarpetals.com
Foundation bras and appliqués

Tribal Bazaar www.tribalbazaar.com
Tribal jewelry and textiles

Sources for Lingerie Bras

Frederick's of Hollywood www.fredericks.com
JC Penny www.jcpenney.com

L'eggs®/Hanes®/Bali®/Playtex® www.onehanesplace.com

Bigger Bras www.biggerbras.com

Fig Leaves www.figleaves.com

References

Lingerie History

Benson, Elaine and John Esten. *Unmentionables: A Brief History of Underwear.* Simon and Shuster: New York 1999.

Cox, Caroline. *Lingerie: A Lexicon of Style.* St. Martin's Press: New York 2000.

Farrell-Beck, Jane and Colleen Gau. *Uplift: The Bra in America.* University of Pennsylvania Press: Philadelphia 2001.

Sewing and Design

Bensussen, Rusty. *Shortcuts to A Perfect Sewing Pattern.* Sterling Publications: New York 1989.

Cox, Caroline. *Lingerie: A Lexicon of Style.* St. Martin's Press: New York 2001.

New Complete Guide to Sewing. Readers Digest Association: New York 2003.

Singer. *Sewing For Special Occasions.* Singer: Minnetonka, MI 1994.

Embellishments

Cambell-Harding, Valerie. *Bead Embroidery.* Lacies: Berkeley 1993.

Clarke, Amy C. and Robin Atkins. *Beaded Embellishment.* Interweave Press: Loveland, CO 2002.

Conlon, Jane. *Fine Embellishment Techniques.* Taunton Press: Newtown, CT 1998.

Ganderton, Lucinda. *Stitch Sampler: The Ultimate Visual Dictionary to Over 200 Classic Stitches.* DK Publishing: London 1999.

Lemon, Jane. *Metal Thread Embroidery: Tools, Materials and Techniques.* Batsford: London 1990.

Valley, Stephanie. *Embellishments A to Z.* Taunton Press: Newtown, CT 1999.

Internet Articles

The Bra Dilemma - Solved! www.taunton.com/threads/pages/t00111.asp

> Article from *Threads* magazine that steps through the process of making a pattern from an existing bra.

Best Fitting Bra. www.electricneedle.com/bra.html

> Directions for making your own pattern for a bra from a basic sloper.

There are many more excellent resources available on Davina's Website.

www.davina.us

Learn more online

Davina's blog and website are a treasure trove of information about all things related to Middle Eastern dance and costuming. Find answers to your costuming questions, informative articles, and photo galleries.

Dawn also produces a quarterly e-zine called *Costumer's Notes.* Every issue is chock-full of editorials, book and magazine reviews, ideas for projects that you can make yourself, hints, tips, and techniques for buying, making, and wearing costumes.

www.davina.us

Publications from Ibexa Press

Ibexa Press is proud to publish and carry Dawn Devine's line of publications. Her other publications include:

Books

- *Embellished Bras: Basic Techniques*
- *Costuming From the Hip*
- *Bedlah, Baubles, and Beads*
- *From Turban to Toe Ring*

eBooks

- *Hints & Tips*
- *Skirting the Issues*
- *Pants for the Dance*
- *Style File: A Visual Vocabulary*

Look for these books from your favorite vendor or order online directly from Ibexa Press.

www.ibexa.com

CPSIA information can be obtained at www.ICGtesting.com
Printed in the USA
BVOW050606090512

289702BV00022B/1/P

9 780615 460529